One of the many beautiful views of Lanzarote, where most of the photographs in this book were taken.

The Keto Cure 2

A new life in 14 days

"What you described: 'A new life in 14 days', has come true. After two weeks, I had lost three kilos, and after four weeks almost five kilos—without feeling hungry! All that while I'm going through menopause. And my guests at the table enjoy the meals as much as I do! The funny thing is my eating habits have really changed. Thank you, Pascale, this was a huge eye-opener for me. Warm regards."

Annushka, a reader

Lannoo

CONTENTS

The recipes in this book are for two people, unless indicated otherwise.
But listen to your body: if you're hungry, eat more. If you're full, stop eating.

All ceramics in the book were designed by Pascale Naessens. Besides being an author she is also a ceramist.

You can find her creations via Pure Tableware by Pascale Naessens for Serax or via her website **www.purepascale.com**

TO BEGIN WITH

Keto is more popular than ever!

Honestly, I hadn't expected *The Keto Cure* to be such a success. It was Belgium's best-selling cookbook in 2020! I was particularly surprised that so many people are interested in this specific diet. Many are wildly enthusiastic, while others are nonplussed. People are enthusiastic because they lose excess weight and particularly because they can continue to eat delicious food and don't feel hungry. The weight loss was spectacular for some people and more subtle for others. This immediately shows how different we all are. The realization that we all react differently to food is steadily growing. That's something I applaud wholeheartedly: it's something I've been drawing attention to ever since my first book.

The idea that we all should eat the same way is outdated and no longer a scientific given. People are becoming increasingly aware that they need to find a way of eating that suits them, both in terms of their bodies and their genetic dispositions.

A Facebook group was set up as a follow-up to the book *The Keto Cure*. If you want to follow a ketogenic diet, I would certainly recommend joining the group; you learn a lot from each other, and you immediately get a sense of what keeps keto enthusiasts busy.

If keto is completely new to you, then I recommend reading *The Keto Cure* first. This book contains the basics and an explanation of what the ketogenic process is, how to get started on your keto journey, the benefits and disadvantages, why it's such a controversial diet, and much more. In *The Keto Cure 2*, we go more in-depth into the questions people have once they start eating keto.

There have also been a lot of questions about intermittent fasting. That's why I've asked Prof. Hanno Pijl, who is himself adept at intermittent fasting, to deal with this topic in-depth. What are the health benefits of intermittent fasting and what's known as time-restricted eating?

And, perhaps the most frequently asked question: "Help, my cholesterol levels increase with keto. Should I be worried?" What's the story with cholesterol? Do high cholesterol levels really lead to cardiovascular disease? What are the latest insights on the subject? That's what I asked Dr. William Cortvriendt. He delved into the recent science on this topic and provides clear answers to these questions.

The Keto Cure 2 is another fascinating book, with a new 14-day keto meal planner and extra recipes for continuing your keto cure so you can once more immerse yourself in the wonderful world of the ketogenic diet.

I wish you an exciting journey full of discovery and inspiration.

Pascale

How do my keto recipes differ from most other recipes?

A varied diet is the best guarantee of a healthy and fit body. That means that you'll find plenty of vegetables, nuts and seeds in my books, but also fish, meat, eggs, cheese and healthy fats, all produced from unprocessed or minimally processed ingredients.
But vegetables continue to form the basis of my recipes. That's perhaps the biggest challenge when developing my keto recipes. It's not easy to create delicious, simple and appealing keto recipes where vegetables take center stage because they are usually rich in carbs, and the whole point is to eat as few carbs as possible.
But vegetables are perhaps even more critical with a ketogenic diet; they're the best source of fiber you have in this case. Fiber is essential for the proper functioning of your gut, your microbiome and your feeling of well-being. Vegetables also provide plenty of vitamins and secondary plant nutrients that all contribute to your health.

As someone who loves to cook, I would like to add that vegetables, above all ingredients, leave room for creativity: they add flavor, color and texture and can be combined to create the most surprising results ...
They make food fun, playful and varied.
That's why I've challenged myself to create recipes that meet all the requirements. Not only are they low on carbs but also include moderate quantities of protein and healthy fats. Because when you eat keto, you should also eat delicious, nutritious and varied foods.

Why do I use existing recipes from other books in *The Keto Cure 2*?

This book contains 50 new recipes and 24 existing recipes, some of them translated into English for the first time. All the recipes have been adjusted to include the right quantities of carbs, fats and protein to reach and remain in ketosis.

I also use existing recipes to show that there are plenty of keto recipes in my other books, even in my very first book.

Once you've gained insight into the difference between keto and moderately low-carb, and where the two systems overlap, you can work with all my books and recipes and use them interchangeably. You can try the keto recipes or the moderately low-carb dishes, or you can "cycle". This gives you access to many more recipes and makes cooking more fun.

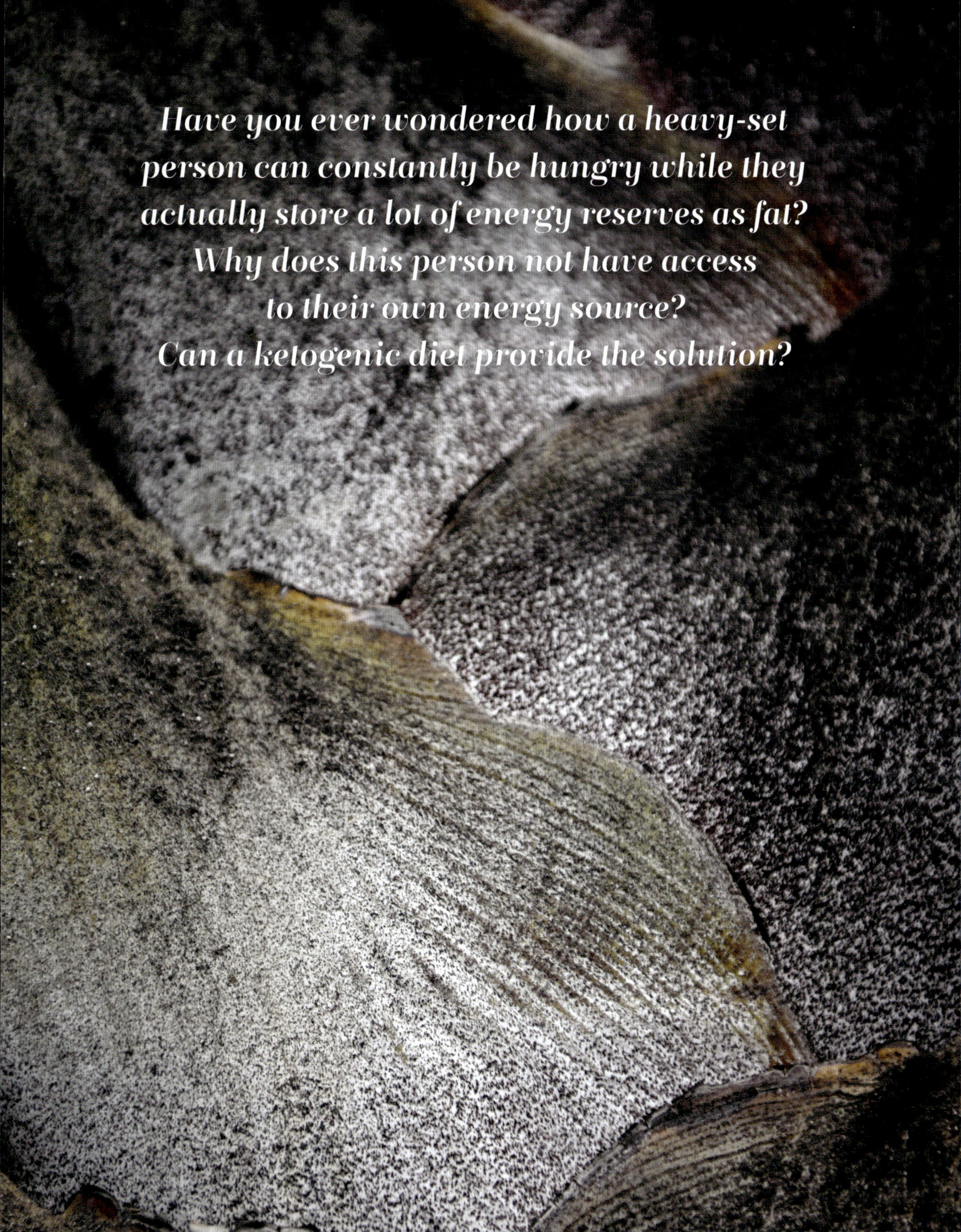

Have you ever wondered how a heavy-set person can constantly be hungry while they actually store a lot of energy reserves as fat? Why does this person not have access to their own energy source? Can a ketogenic diet provide the solution?

THEORY: HOW IT WORKS

What is a ketogenic diet? A summary

When you follow a ketogenic diet, you eat so few carbs (starches and sugars), less than 30 grams a day, that your body is forced to switch from burning sugars to burning fats. Once your body starts burning lots of fats —whether that's your own body fat or fats from your diet—your body will start to produce ketones, which act as a type of replacement fuel. When ketones become your most important source of energy, you're in ketosis.
By eating in this way, you teach your body to efficiently burn fat as an energy source.
What's more, after a while, your body will choose fats over glucose as its fuel source. In so doing, the body will draw on its fat reserves, causing you to lose weight if you're overweight. Another benefit is that your body has access to a larger energy store because a human being can store more fat than glucose. That's why many athletes like to experiment with a ketogenic diet.

That doesn't mean that glucose doesn't play a role. When you're in ketosis, your body produces its glucose from proteins and fats. Just enough to provide certain cell types, such as red blood cells that can only burn glucose, with enough energy. Moreover, you're always taking in a very small quantity of carbs through what you eat.

Nutritional ketosis is a natural metabolic state. It's a side effect of the natural human tendency to create and burn ketones as a source of energy when carbs (starches and sugars) are not readily available. Throughout history that has enabled us to deal with changes in food supply and food scarcity. Depending on the season, the hunt and the location, more or less food was available at any given time.

Being able to switch between two systems —burning sugars and burning fats—was and is a natural process that provides many health benefits. But, with the rise of the agricultural and food industries, we started to eat more and more carbs. With this constant supply of excessive carbs, our bodies don't get around to properly burning off stored fats; our bodies have forgotten how to optimally burn "fats" as a source of energy.

Several health benefits are associated with the eating of fewer carbohydrates and more fats:

- weight loss (including belly fat)
- breaking through a weight plateau
- less hunger
- no more uncontrollable food cravings
- no blood sugar spikes or drops
- greater clarity of mind
- improved cholesterol and triglyceride levels
- improved sleep (usually)
- improved condition for people with type 2 diabetes (although they should always be guided by professionals as their medication needs to be adjusted to prevent hypos).
- positive effect on high blood pressure
- positive effect on people with insulin resistance (lower blood glucose levels and improved insulin sensitivity)
- more stamina (because you have access to your larger fat reserves as opposed to your limited glycogen reserves)

Important! The ketogenic diet and medication

Nutritional ketosis through diet is a powerful tool to lose weight and counter certain conditions such as type 2 diabetes. But it can also be dangerous, especially when you take medication that isn't adjusted to match your new eating habits. Anyone taking medication should never start a ketogenic diet without consulting a healthcare professional first. In particular, I'm referring to people with type 1 or type 2 diabetes, people with liver or kidney conditions and people with high blood pressure who are on medication. The biggest changes occur during the first few days of the diet, and that's when adjustments need to be made. The good thing is that it reduces your medicine intake, but if you don't and you eat keto, serious health issues may develop as a result. I recommend that everyone first read extensively about what a ketogenic diet involves, so you know what you're getting yourself into.

- positive effect on conditions such as epilepsy, with research currently being conducted into the positive effects of a ketogenic diet with Alzheimer's and certain types of cancer

I'm an absolute proponent of a temporary ketogenic diet; that's why I see it as a cure. When alternated with a moderately low-carb way of eating, you'll get all the health benefits, plus a lot of flexibility and freedom.

Would you like professional guidance? On my website, www.purepascale.com, you'll find a list of professionals.

Why does the ketogenic diet work?

The ketogenic diet often works where other diets have failed because:

1. It's a type of diet that involves "eating". You can eat delicious, high-quality and even fatty foods without calorie restrictions, and your body still feels satisfied.
2. Ketones reduce your appetite.
3. Because you eat very few carbs, your blood sugar levels remain highly stable, so you no longer feel hungry or get food cravings.

Eating keto means "dieting through eating". Satisfaction plays a key role

Despite the controversy, for me neither proponents nor opponents can get around the keto success stories; many people lose weight with it. Still, it's not a suitable diet for everyone because it's quite strict. But for some, this feels like a liberation; they finally manage to lose weight without going hungry.

Some people—and professionals—still want to hold on to the classic vision of dieting: "Eat less (particularly less fat) and exercise more." But my biggest problem with that is: do they really think that people who start a keto diet haven't tried that already? Heavy-set people often have an entire history of following those kinds of calorie-restrictive diets. The well-meaning advice "Eat less and exercise more" doesn't work for everyone. In fact, I don't think it works for most people —why else would so many people be overweight? Many people get even hungrier when they follow the fat-free advice, causing them to eat more and gain weight instead. They then use all their will-power to try and keep to the calorie restrictions and fight hunger. Still, it's a fight you always lose in the end because your body will always win out over your mind at some point. Anyone who is constantly hungry will never succeed in any kind of diet. Your body will force you to eat until it's satisfied.

The key here is "satisfaction". You need to make sure that your body is truly satiated so that your body (your gut and your stomach) sends messages to the brain saying: "I've eaten enough. I'm full." Only then will you stop eating. The balance between hunger, eating, and satisfaction isn't a matter of choice. Your body decides for you. It's mainly an interplay between hormones, and you and your willpower have very little to say about that, no matter how much willpower you have. You can keep it up for a while, but not in the long term. So, each diet's success is dependent on how satisfied you feel. Anyone who is satiated—you know, that pleasant feeling of being full without having eaten too much—will stop eating.[1]

You can see an excellent example of how satisfaction works with children. Their eyes are often bigger than their stomachs. They pile food on their plates or ask for more, and then suddenly they're full and can't eat another bite. They would like to eat more, but their body says that it's had enough. If you then force your child to eat everything left on their plate, they'll start to gag. When your body, mind and hormones are in balance, that satiated feeling is very powerful.

A ketogenic diet doesn't revolve around eating less or restricting calories (although that's sometimes what it comes down to), but about eating differently. The ketogenic diet was initially developed for epilepsy patients. It was discovered that once epilepsy patients started to fast, they were less prone to seizures. But, because people can't fast forever, a diet that mimicked fasting was developed. That's how the ketogenic diet was born. Researchers established that, when you follow a diet rich in fats and low in carbohydrates, you can achieve more or less the same effects as fasting. But with the huge advantage that your body doesn't go into hibernation mode, which it does when you follow a crash diet or a diet with a long-term calorie restriction.

1 People with an eating disorder often have a hormone imbalance. Moreover, psychological and genetic aspects often play a role, completely throwing that satiated feeling off-balance. In that case, we recommended you find a professional with extensive nutritional expertise who is open to new insights on nutrition and health.

The last thing you want is for your body to go into hibernation mode because then your body will draw on what you eat more than usual. This means you'll gain weight while eating less. But the biggest problem is that those hormonal changes are still there a year later. Anyone following a crash diet or restricting their calories for longer periods ends up in a position where they have to eat even less, gain weight even more quickly and end up with even greater hunger pangs.
It's a typical downward spiral where many overweight people end up—the harder they try, the more weight they gain—that's just really unfair!
That's why a ketogenic diet can often provide a solution for this group of people: they're allowed to eat delicious food, the hungry feeling goes away, in part because fat satiates, and their body doesn't go into hibernation mode. On the contrary, they have more energy, feel great and lose weight.

Ketones suppress hunger

When sugars (carbs) are not available, your body produces more ketones as a fuel source. Ketones are excellent fuel for your body and your brain because they release less oxidative stress and free radicals during the conversion process, and they have anti-inflammatory properties. In other words, they're a "cleaner" fuel source than glucose. One important additional positive effect of ketones is that they suppress hunger. Studies conducted with mice has proven this to be the case, and perhaps the same applies to people.

But it's not, "the more ketones, the better"

It's interesting to note that your body always produces ketones, even with a carbohydrate-rich diet. However, in normal circumstances, ketone levels are never higher than 0.5 mmol/l. Nutritional ketosis (ketosis reached through nutrition) occurs when ketone levels of between 0.5 and 3 mmol/l are measured. That is an optimal concentration at which ketones are the most efficient at providing energy to your brain, muscles and organs. Higher values, between 3 and 5 mmol/l can occur just after strenuous exercise—because then you've used up all your glycogen (sugars in your muscles) and your body is fueling itself with extra energy in the form of ketones—or when you're fasting (for more information, see Prof. Hanno Pijl's contribution in this book on page 39). When values reach between 5 and 10 mmol/l, we're talking about "starvation ketosis". You'll never reach higher values, around 10 mmol/l, with nutrition or fasting alone. These levels indicate insulin production problems, and then we're talking about "ketoacidosis", a dangerous condition where the ketones accumulate in the body and acidify the blood. This condition is rare, but it can be fatal. Ketoacidosis occurs in patients with untreated type 1 diabetes. *The Keto Cure* book explains how you can measure your ketone levels.

So it's not, "the more ketones, the better". When it comes to losing weight or putting type 2 diabetes into remission, values between 0.5 and 3 (up to 5) mmol/l are ideal. Then you can enjoy the health benefits of a ketogenic diet and experience less hunger. Many professionals also agree that it's not so much about the ketone levels, but about the lifestyle: fewer (fast) carbs, more fat and moderate quantities of protein.

Tip: a practical approach to ketone levels

In the beginning, you're curious and want to be able to measure your ketone levels right away. You want to know: am I on the right track? And it's fun; the ketone levels seem like some kind of reward. But once you're more accustomed to the ketogenic diet, you don't feel the need to measure your levels all the time. Would you like to measure your ketone levels? Here are a couple of tips: don't use MCT oils or external ketones just before measuring your ketone levels. Your ketone concentration is usually lower in the mornings than in the evenings and fluctuates during the day, depending on your activity levels and what you eat. If your levels are between 0.5 and 3 mmol/l, then you're right on target. If you measure higher levels, you're not eating or drinking enough (or perhaps you're fasting?). You can also measure higher levels after strenuous exercise. If your measurement is around or higher than 10 mmol/l, consult your physician immediately.
There's still a lot of controversy around exogenic ketones. These ketones are produced outside your body and are consumed from external sources. Do they offer the same health benefits as endogenic or ketones produced by your body? Do exogenic ketones suppress the production of endogenic ketones? In short, the idea of "the more ketones, the better" certainly doesn't apply here.

Blood sugar levels remain stable during a ketogenic diet

Peaking and dropping sugar and insulin levels drive hunger and fat accumulation

Your body is not a machine that functions perfectly every single second. If you eat lots of (fast) carbs, your body will detect "lots of sugar". This triggers a whole series of reactions that include stimulating the production of insulin, the hormone that removes sugar from your blood and makes sure it gets to your muscles or is converted into fat. So when you eat lots of fast carbs, your body reacts quite strongly. Too much insulin is produced, causing your blood sugar levels to dip, giving you that hungry feeling and hankering for something sweet, those dreaded "cravings". This is your body's way of saying that it wants to stock up on glucose because your body wants to keep its blood sugar levels constant between its upper and lower limits.
So you've just eaten a lot of food, but you still end up feeling hungry. That's why meals that contain a lot of fast carbs briefly leave you feeling satisfied, only to find that you're hungry in no time.

Another problem: our bodies can only stock up on a limited supply of glucose (some in the muscles and some in the liver) as glycogen. Once those stores are full, the surplus carbs you eat are immediately converted into fat.

You've become a real fat-producing machine, and, what's worse, you're constantly hungry because you need to keep replenishing your limited sugar supply. Sadly enough, during this entire process, your body completely ignores the body fat you've already stored. And to top it all off, your fat reserves are increased every time you eat too many carbs.

You end up in a vicious circle when you consume more (fast) carbs than you burn: peaking and dropping sugar and insulin levels drive hunger and fat accumulation.

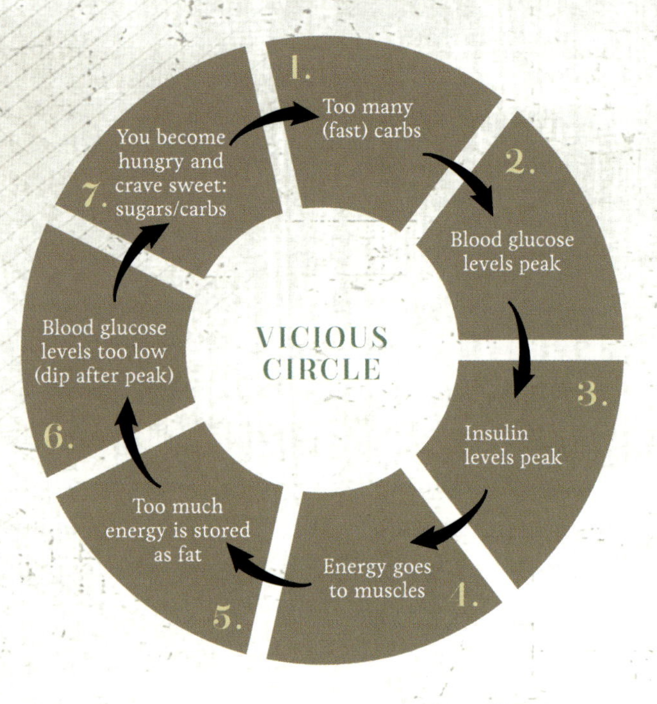

Would you like to break the vicious circle? Then you'll need to force your body to start burning fats instead of sugars, and you do that by denying yourself almost all sugars (carbs).

The ketogenic diet gets this derailed process back on track as it were:

- it turns you into an effective fat-burner;
- it stabilizes your blood sugar and insulin levels (less hunger and fewer cravings);
- it breaks the vicious circle of hunger and fat accumulation.

You can see a keto cure as rebooting your body. You teach your body to work with "fat" as an energy source.

How can you lose weight while eating so much and so many calories?

The idea that losing weight is as simple as "count your fat, protein and carb calories each day and make sure they're less than what you use up in a day" is too simplistic. The body is much more complex than that. Proteins, fats and carbs all trigger different hormonal reactions, which in turn affect our metabolisms, and our sensations of hunger and satisfaction. So the idea that a calorie is just a calorie, irrespective of where it comes from, no longer applies; fat-rich diets have proven that already. But that doesn't mean calories don't play a role. On the contrary, we're increasingly seeing that you end up eating less than you think with a ketogenic diet, mainly because what you do eat is so filling.

In other words: if you eat too much, you will gain weight, even when you're on a ketogenic diet. Losing weight is still a matter of having an energy deficit even when you're on a ketogenic diet. Therefore, a ketogenic diet doesn't give you carte blanche to eat as much fat as you want. (See the paragraph on "How much fat" on page 20)
The reason you lose weight with a ketogenic diet is not completely clear yet; there is still a lot of controversy around it. But the aspects below play a central role:

- You'll feel hungry less often because ketones, fats and proteins are more filling than carbs. So you'll eventually end up eating less than you think with a ketogenic diet.
- Your body produces less insulin, the hormone that's known to store fat.
- People who eat keto are in optimal condition for burning fats; your body will more burn fat rather than storing it. According to Dr. Stephen Pinney, fat-adapted people burn twice as much fat as people following a traditional diet.
- The research conducted by Professor David Ludwig is fascinating. He has shown that people burn more energy when they follow a diet rich in fats and low in carbs than when they follow a diet rich in carbs and low in fats. Especially after two weeks, when you've become fat-adapted.
- You can eat more with a low-carb, fat-rich diet without gaining weight because your body generally uses up more energy. This translates into feeling "energetic" and fit.[2]

One reader hit the nail right on the head when she wrote: "I've been trying to lose weight by cutting my calories (and fats) for years. I felt listless and had no energy, even the simplest of stretching exercises wore me out. I went keto and lost 30 kilos. The pain was gone, my skin improved, and I had more energy.
Keto turned my life around. It's a complete paradigm shift. It's clear that your body undergoes a fundamental and systemic change, something that's better adapted to your endocrine system than the "calorie in/out" model."

Why I'm a proponent of a keto diet and of "cycling" your diet

What is cycling?

I've received quite a few reactions because I'm not a proponent of following a ketogenic diet long-term. Some see keto as a lifestyle, a way of eating that they want to continue for the rest of their lives. Although I fully subscribe to the benefits of a ketogenic diet, I'm absolutely not a fan of a long-term ketogenic diet; but I am a fan of "cycling", or switching between keto and low-carb. I adhere to the scientific school of thought that shows, on evolutionary grounds, that people have always been omnivores who also consume carbs. In addition, following a ketogenic diet over the long-term can lead to a shortage in dietary fiber, which is essential for a healthy microbiome.

2 Source: https://academic.oup.com/jn/advance-article/doi/10.1093/jn/nxaa350/6020167

As I said earlier, a ketogenic diet mimics a type of fasting, and it's never a good idea to fast for long periods. Each form of fasting has health benefits, especially in the beginning, but not in the long term. Moreover, if you think the western diet contains extreme amounts of carbs, then you can't see the ketogenic diet in any other way than extremely high in fats and extremely low in carbs. It doesn't make sense to start demonizing carbs instead of fats. Extremes lead to extremes.

You want to make and keep your body flexible; variation is a fundamental biological principle to get the most out of what nature has to offer. Our bodies have the flexibility to adapt, but by eating the same thing for long periods, the body loses that ability to adjust. By changing your eating patterns, your body remains alert.

Many die-hard keto adepts have changed their minds about being in long-term ketosis because occasionally eating "healthy" carbs also has its benefits. People feel good about eating them, and it offers more variation in their diet. With long-term keto nutrition, you miss out on the benefits of eating fruits, vegetables and root vegetables and are short on vitamins (potassium in particular), secondary plant-based nutrients and fibers that benefit your gut bacteria.

It's much more important to understand how it works and to reap the benefits from the two different systems, burning fats and burning sugars. That's why I'm a big proponent of cycling. By that, I mean periods of keto switched with periods of low-carb. You're still staying away from fast carbs such as bread, pasta, rice and potatoes. Let me be clear about this: I don't recommend switching between keto and "high" carb, eating lots of (fast) carbs.

The point is not to gorge on fries, cake and cookies on the weekend and go keto during the week. That is challenging your body to switch between extremes. Which is not going to make you feel better; on the contrary.[3] In addition, you're not creating new eating habits, which is a recipe for failure. But cycling between keto and low-carb offers many advantages, not only for your health because you eat a more varied diet, but you also feel less restricted in your choices, which means it's easier to keep up.

3 Some athletes do actually go to these extremes, but that's done very consciously and carefully. They train to ketogenic extremes and then eat plenty of (fast) carbs such as rice. Their muscles have first used up all the glycogen, or sugar, in their bodies, causing them to act like a sponge and suck up all those ingested sugars. The result, especially with protein, leads to maximum muscle enhancement—literally bulging muscles—because glycogen contains more moisture. Athletes that work in this way can and are allowed to eat (fast) carbs because they have already used up all the carbs in their bodies during their intensive training. At that moment, the carbs they eat aren't "too much"; enough to replenish their muscle glycogen levels, but not enough to start storing fats. They use both systems, the fat and sugar burning system, and take the best from both. They teach their bodies to get the most from burning fats and enjoy the benefits of having glucose in their muscles. Before you decide to try this yourself, remember, it involves really intense, heavy training. :-)

So the question remains: why would you want to stay in ketosis if you can reap many of the same health benefits from a moderately low-carb way of eating, such as weight loss (when you're overweight), more energy, a clear mind, stable insulin and blood sugar levels ...

Before you start cycling, you first need to become fat-adapted. This means that your body will choose fat over glucose as a source of energy. You do this by following a strict keto diet for at least 14 days or three weeks. Then you gradually switch to a moderately low-carb way of eating. Your body will still burn fats optimally.

Possible ways to cycle

There are many ways you can cycle your diets. You can, for example, go keto during the week and switch to low-carb on the weekends. Or you can generally eat low-carb and throw in a week of keto here and there. Or keep switching between keto and low-carb like I do. First of all, I choose quality food. I don't consciously say, "Okay, now I'm going to eat low-carb," or "now I'm going to eat keto." On the days that I don't have fruit for breakfast, or just some berries with full-fat yogurt and nuts (like I do in the summer), or a hearty breakfast with eggs, and I eat few carbs in the afternoon or evening, I'm in a mild state of ketosis in no time. I always eat low-carb, and sometimes that happens to be keto, and sometimes it doesn't. I don't plan anything. I just eat what I feel like, but I seldom or never eat fast carbs.

There is a difference between nutritional ketosis and medicinal ketosis

Most people follow a ketogenic diet to lose weight. That's what we call nutritional ketosis. Some people choose or must follow a ketogenic diet for health reasons, in which case we call it medicinal ketosis. One example is epilepsy patients, for whom the diet was initially developed. Research is also currently being conducted into the health benefits for Alzheimer and cancer patients. The ketogenic diet can have a beneficial effect on some types of cancer, but not all, and this field still requires a lot of research. In those cases, patients are always monitored medically.

How much fat, protein and carbs am I allowed to eat while following a ketogenic diet?

How many carbs am I allowed to eat while following a ketogenic diet?

The answer to this is straightforward: as many as you want without falling out of ketosis. For most people, that's between 30 and 50 grams of carbohydrates per day. The more insulin-resistant you are, the harder it is to reach ketosis and the fewer carbs you're allowed to eat. Once you're fat-adapted and your body has adjusted to optimal fat burning, you can eat slightly more carbs. You can also eat slightly more carbs after exercise. Which carbs you should eat are discussed in *The Keto Cure*.

How much fat am I allowed to eat while following a ketogenic diet?

With keto, you're allowed to be generous with fat. Still, I've noticed that some people in our "Keto Cure" Facebook group were a bit too generous with fat; they were adding extra fat to everything, and that's taking it a bit too far. What role do fats play in a ketogenic diet? First and foremost, you should know that it's not the extra fats that help you reach ketosis but the absence of carbs. Fasting, together with training, is probably the fastest way to reach ketosis, and that doesn't involve eating fats.

So why should we eat more fats while following a ketogenic diet?

We take away practically all carbs, so we need to eat something else to replace them. Otherwise, you would eat very little, be constantly hungry, and give up in no time. So we replace the carbs with fats, and that works out well because we want your body to burn fats—and your own body fat with it.

People who are in ketosis burn twice as much fat as usual. However, if you take in too much fat, you will never get around to using up your fat reserves, and you won't lose weight. If you take in too little fat, your body will start to break down its muscles to get the energy it needs. See fat as your new source of energy.

And, as with everything else, finding the right balance is key. If you want to lose weight and you're not losing weight, use a little less fat. If you don't have to lose weight, you can consume a little more fat. But the goal is not to eat extra fats; just eat the fats that are part of a full nutritional diet. If your piece of meat has fat on it, don't cut it away, but eat it instead. Use milk products that have not been skimmed, such as full-fat yogurts and cheeses. Don't be afraid to eat fat-rich products such as nuts, fatty fish, avocados ... And you can be generous with olive oil. Use fat as a flavor enhancer and to give you that full feeling.

Which fats?

The idea is that, just like with everything in your diet, you vary your fat intake. Polyunsaturated fats are essential. We usually consume more than enough omega-6 fats, so concentrate on the omega-3 fats found in fish and shellfish. These fats are exceptionally good for your heart, your brain and cell generation, have anti-inflammatory properties, and are promoted by scientists researching longevity.

The following may surprise you: the fats that can be most quickly converted into energy are the mono-unsaturated fats, found in olive oil, for example, and saturated fats, which you find in butter, coconut oil, full-fat yogurt or cream, but also in bacon (which is half saturated and half mono-unsaturated fat).

So olive oil continues to be a first-class ingredient in this diet. And you don't need to be afraid of saturated fats.

Once you're fat-adapted, you use twice as much fat as an energy source as you used to. These fats are not stored in the body (unless you eat too much fat), and they don't clog up your arteries;

they provide an accessible energy source.
If you're eating keto and eating so many fats makes you feel uncomfortable, check which fats you're eating. According to Dr. Stephen Phinney, it's often the omega-6 fats that cause the problem, such as mayonnaise with sunflower or corn oil, dressings with soy oil, peanut oils ...

If I eat so many saturated fats, what does that do to the fat levels in my blood?

Oddly enough, the blood fat levels improve with a ketogenic diet. During one study conducted by several scientists, including Dr. Stephen Phinney, people were monitored for a year. The people following a ketogenic diet saw their triglyceride levels and cholesterol profile improve. This is contrary to everything we've been taught so far. Even though you eat more fat and more saturated fats, your blood fat levels improve during a ketogenic diet, especially once you're fat-adapted.
The saturated fats and cholesterol you consume do not directly correlate to your blood's saturated fat and cholesterol levels. With a ketogenic diet, you mostly burn saturated fat. That's your new source of energy. It's an entirely different story when you eat plenty of carbs and lots of saturated fat. A recent study has proven that it's not so much your LDL cholesterol levels that are the primary indicator for your risk of developing cardiovascular disease, but your metabolic health, so things like how overweight you are, type 2 diabetes, high blood pressure, fat and cholesterol profile ...[4]

This is a major hot topic that deserves more attention. That's why I've asked expert Dr. William Cortvriendt to delve into the scientific research and outline the story behind saturated fats and cholesterol, given what we know now, as plenty of studies have been conducted in this field recently. Read more about his findings on page 50.

How much protein am I allowed to eat while following a ketogenic diet?

Some low-carb diets are high in protein and low in fat. How healthy are they? Are they less, more, or just as effective for generating weight loss? There is still a lot of controversy around this. Part of the reason is that proteins, just like carbs, raise your insulin levels, although to a lesser degree than carbs (fat only causes a minimal rise in insulin levels). Some scientists believe you can't become a good fat burner if you have higher insulin levels. For the same reasons, people who are insulin-resistant and therefore have more insulin in their blood have a more challenging time reaching ketosis. The reason for that is that insulin stimulates fat storage instead of the combustion of fat.
Another argument for being careful with excessive protein consumption—but again, the jury is still out on this—is that when you eat lots of protein, it spontaneously triggers gluconeogenesis.
This means that your body starts producing its own glucose from proteins and fats in the absence of carbs. Because even when you're in ketosis, your body needs some glucose to function well.

4 Source: https://jamanetwork.com/journals/jamacardiology/article-abstract/2775559

However, too much protein could encourage gluconeogenesis too much and make you fall out of ketosis. The question is whether that is indeed the case. Many keto adepts, especially athletes and bodybuilders, eat more protein and are very enthusiastic about the results.
To sum up, more research clearly needs to be conducted regarding this aspect.
But you want to avoid a high-protein diet for another reason: proteins encourage all sorts of processes in the body that are linked to ageing, cardiovascular conditions and cancer. Proteins stimulate growth, but once you're an adult, you don't want to grow old. In fact, you want to reduce this ageing process as much as possible. :-)

What everyone does agree on is that proteins are the most filling nutrients. They play an essential role in building and repairing your body. So consuming enough protein is very important.
Your body cannot produce most amino acids (the building blocks of proteins), so you need to ingest them through nutrition. That's why they're called "essential".

The amount of protein also continues to be a hot topic in mainstream healthcare. Current guidelines state that 0.8 grams of protein for every 1 kg of body weight is ideal. A standard keto diet uses slightly higher protein levels, between 1 and 1.3 grams protein per kilogram.
But Dr. Stephen Pinney, one of the founders of the modern keto diet, even mentions 1.5 grams of protein per kilogram of body weight. He recommends not going below 1.2 grams or over 2 grams per kilogram of body weight (based on the ideal weight).

Conclusion: proteins

My idea is that you shouldn't be too worried about all the numbers. I'm not a fan of keeping track of all those macronutrients; just knowing the principles behind them should be enough. We are all different, and we all have different lifestyles, so our needs vary as well. There's no magic formula.

My suggestion is: follow the recipes as indicated in the book and see how that feels. If you feel good, don't change anything. This will probably be the case for most people. But know that eating slightly more protein (the same applies to eating carbs) can make the difference between feeling great and feeling miserable. In that case, it's a good idea to lower your fat intake slightly, especially if losing weight is your goal. The challenge with a ketogenic diet is to consume enough protein to meet all your needs, but not overdoing it.

Some reasons to increase your protein intake during a ketogenic diet (by eating more fish or a larger piece of meat) are:
- you don't feel well, and you're stressed out;
- you practise a lot of sports;
- you train a lot and want to develop muscle tissue;
- you're hungry all the time;
- you're stuck on a weight plateau.

To track or not to track macros?

Trust your body instead of your calculator

A ketogenic diet is low in carbs, moderate in proteins and high in fat. In the beginning, it might be helpful to keep track of your macros to help you gain insight into what you eat. That means that you note down how many carbs and how much fat and protein you eat every day. But at some point, you're going to have to let this go, so you have more time for the fun things in life.

Know that the calculations in this book (as in all books) are just an indication, so don't pin yourself down to these figures. The results differ depending on which source or app you use. Look up eggplant or tomato in three different carb charts, and you'll get three different figures. These calculations have already led to a lot of discussions. Also, bear in mind that if a recipe calls for "2 tablespoons olive oil", you won't always consume everything because fat is often left in the pan after frying. Or, I often cook vegetables with a generous splash of olive oil, but some of that oil gets poured down the drain together with any excess water. That makes calculating the exact figures a bit problematic.

I refuse to reduce cooking to an exact science, even with keto. Moreover, cooking should always be an intuitive process; this allows you to connect with your body, which is critical. Our bodies are not machines into which we stuff the necessary nutrients in theoretically ideal proportions and then just press a button. That's not how it works. We are also human beings filled with emotions, not forgetting the social element. There are so many factors that you can't control. You'll be hungrier one day than the next and more active on one day than another. This all influences how and how much we eat. Anyone who refuses to take in the whole picture will quit sooner or later.

That's also why I prefer to talk in terms of a generous splash of olive oil or a knob of butter rather than so many teaspoonfuls of oil or so many grams of butter. That leaves room for your personal touch; if you're hungry, you'll automatically make that splash a bit more generous, and if you're not a big eater, you'll add less. I think that personal touch is essential! That's the only way to gain insight into your own body.

I understand it may be helpful for some people to keep track of their macros. You learn to figure out how many carbs foods contain, and that can lead to some surprising and useful insights. But once you've gained that insight, I would recommend that you cook intuitively.

Learn to trust your body. If you want to lose weight and you're not succeeding, use less fat. Find out where the balance lies; this is different for everyone. Learn to cook using yourself as a guide. If you want more vegetables, add more. If you want fewer vegetables, add less. Cooking should be fun, and the idea that you can measure everything is an illusion.

Experience, and above all, enjoy!

The numbers approach

I've debated whether to provide this example, but maybe this will offer some insight into how keto works. I've calculated a typical example. In Belgium and the Netherlands, we assume that a woman needs 2000 kilocalories each day and that a man needs 2500 kilocalories. With a ketogenic diet, between 5% and 10% of your daily energy comes from carbs, between 15% and 30% comes from proteins and between 60% and 70% comes from fats.

This amounts to:

	Carbohydrates		Proteins		Fats	
	5%	10%	15%	30%	60%	70%
2000 kcal	25 g	50 g	75 g	150 g	133 g	156 g
2500 kcal	31 g	63 g	94 g	188 g	167 g	194 g

1 g carbohydrates = 4 kilocalories

1 g proteins = 4 kilocalories

1 g fats = 9 kilocalories

2000 kcal = 5% from carbohydrates = 100 kcal : 4 = 25 g carbohydrates

2000 kcal = 15% from proteins = 300 kcal : 4 = 75 g proteins

2000 kcal = 60% from fats = 1200 kcal : 9 = 133 g fats

Depending on your base metabolism, how active you are and what your goal is (losing weight, maintaining weight or developing muscle tissue), you determine the proportions of your macros.

The intuitive approach

Don't count calories, and don't keep track of your macros. Instead:

- Focus on keeping your carb intake as minimal as possible and eat lots of low-carb vegetables so you can reach and stay in ketosis.
- Keep the portions of your protein sources, such as meat, fish and cheese, about the same as you're used to.
- Don't be afraid to use fats but don't go overboard with them either. Eat as much as you need until you're full, and eat the fats that come naturally with the food. For instance, don't cut away the fatty edges from your lamb chops, but eat them. Cook with fatty foods such as olive oil, fatty fish, avocado, nuts, full-fat yogurt, full-fat cream ...

Think about what you eat (quality) and not about how much you eat (quantity). Learn to understand your hunger and eat until you're full. Reconnect with your body and trust your instincts.

Moreover, people who are used to eating plenty of carbs are surprised at how filling keto dishes can be. They don't recognize that feeling of being truly satiated anymore. So it's not a crime to leave some food lying on your plate. If you're full, stop eating.

The benefit of a fully worked-out meal plan from *The Keto Cure* and *The Keto Cure 2*

With these fully worked-out meal plans, you don't need to worry about what and how much you eat at all. The recipes contain the right quantities of macros to help you reach ketosis and stay there. My advice is: eat until you've had enough. If it's not enough, make more; if it's too much, make less next time or use less fat. You can especially play around with the fat content: use a bit more or less until you have enough. But don't leave the table feeling hungry, and don't restrict your calories.

Athletes and macros

Some top-class athletes keep a close eye on their macros to optimize their performance. If you function at the top of your game, the details make all the difference. Athletes are usually followed by a nutrition expert who monitors and tweaks their intake. Some amateur athletes like to emulate their role models and focus on their macros as well. And if that's what you like to do, there's nothing wrong with that; on the contrary. But I don't think that's the main goal of most people following a ketogenic diet.

Sports and keto

Many athletes train with keto, so their bodies are optimally geared towards burning fats. After all, the fat reserves in your body are far greater than your glycogen (sugar) reserves. Endurance athletes in particular experience the benefits because they no longer reach the point that they use up their limited glycogen store—often described as hitting the wall—but instead have access to a far larger energy store: their body fat. Still, burning glucose is an important process for many athletes. They try to get the best of both worlds to develop their strength and muscle tissue.

It takes a while before your body performs as well on fats as it does on carbs. If you want to lose weight and feel fit, two to three weeks of keto should be enough. If you want to increase your athletic performance, the adjustment may take longer, between three and four weeks, or even a couple of months, according to some experts. The result is that the athlete will perform less well during their adjustment phase from sugar to fat burning. Once the athlete is fully fat-adapted, their performance will improve. In the sports world, extensive research is being carried out with exogenous ketones.

How about dessert?

A dessert once in a while is fine, but don't see it as a full-fledged meal

Once you've gone through the fat-adaptation phase and you know you're on your way to what you want to achieve, you can enjoy the occasional fatty dessert. For most people, that's after they've followed a strict ketogenic diet for two or three weeks. Enjoying your food is important. The desserts from this book are delicious, just like a dessert should be. :-) And thankfully, keto allows for this; it's one of the reasons why the ketogenic diet is so successful. But some people have taken this too far; they turn desserts into meals: keto waffles for breakfast, keto pancakes for lunch, keto cookies as a snack, and keto cake in the evenings, all sweetened with sweeteners. This goes against all logic with regards to healthy nutrition! It's doomed to fail because it won't work in the long term.

Why this doesn't work:

- You end up eating the same ingredients all the time, particularly ground nuts. Ground nuts are not a whole-food product because they're ground; they are a refined product, and because it goes down so easily, you tend to eat a lot of it.
- You maintain your craving for "sweet", so you're not tackling the root of the problem.
- They're still not the real thing. Those pancakes will never taste as good as the original, so you're left with an unfulfilled need that keeps growing.
- You're not changing your eating habits or trying out new flavors. On the contrary, you're eating more desserts than you used to. And for many of us, eating too many sweets is what drives our overweight in the first place.
- In short, you won't be able to keep this up, and you'll revert to your old eating habits.

The challenge is to create delicious keto recipes using "real food", recognizable and nutritious ingredients. Of course, you can treat yourself to a dessert once in a while, sweetened with erythritol if you wish. Enjoy it when you do. Try "mindful" eating: sit down, take your time, be aware of what you eat and enjoy all that delicious food you've prepared. It will literally and figuratively leave you feeling more fulfilled.

Intermittent fasting

"Intermittent fasting", you've probably heard the term before, and many people combine this with keto. But why should you "not" want to eat? Is it healthy, and does it help you lose weight?

I don't personally participate in intermittent fasting or time-restricted eating, but I am convinced that it has health benefits if you do it properly. That's why I've asked Professor Hanno Pijl to write an extensive article on the topic. Not only because, as an endocrinologist, he's researching intermittent fasting at the Leiden University Medical Center, but because he and his wife regularly practise intermittent fasting. He is the ideal person to tell us more about the fascinating world of autophagy, hormesis and intermittent fasting. See page 39 for his article.

If you are considering intermittent fasting, read my personal story first. Just the word "fasting" makes me cringe because years ago, that's how my eating issues started. After a five-day fasting or juice period, I always had such an insatiable hunger that I would eat everything I came across, particularly fast carbs such as bread, spice cake, spaghetti and baked goods: foods that are soft, sweet, and are gone before you know it. The scene was set for completely messing up my hormonal balance. The yo-yo effect dominated my life, and it kept getting worse. For a few years, I had to battle against my eating habits. I'm not implying that fasting was the cause of my eating issues. I'm convinced that when an eating disorder is involved, it's a combination of several different factors and that there's a genetic component involved that makes you susceptible to eating disorders. Some people will never develop an eating disorder, even under the strictest of fasts. But it did help trigger mine, and I don't think I will ever fast; my deep-rooted fear has never really gone away. Some people say that you're less hungry if you fast according to the rules, but I think that's glossing over the issue. Everyone I know who practises fasting, and by that I mean at least 24 hours at a stretch, experiences hunger. But some people are better able to deal with it than others. I know that my body reacts very strongly to real hunger, and that's why I don't practise intermittent fasting. What I don't do is eat all the time; I actually only eat at mealtimes.

Skipping breakfast?

Let's be honest, that's not really fasting. That's what we call time-restricted eating. And that works in favor of most people. You don't have to cook in the mornings. And you usually don't feel like it either; preparing a keto breakfast takes more time than preparing a traditional breakfast. Moreover, you're less hungry when you're in ketosis. So skipping breakfast is something I'd be able to manage. :-) Still, it's not something I tend to do because I don't have a good reason to do so. My health and body weight is on track, so why should I? I feel that I'm in balance in how I live, eat, exercise and enjoy life. And, above all, I fully enjoy the luxury of my husband Paul making breakfast for us. :-) For me, eating is a social event that I love to enjoy with others. Those are the moments I treasure. That's why I try to combine eating delicious, healthy food and enjoying life. :-) The idea of "not eating" makes me rebellious and unhappy. But that's my story, and thankfully we're all different.

However, I'm convinced that skipping a meal can help to lose weight. At least, if you do it the right way and make sure that you eat healthily and don't stuff yourself when you are allowed to eat. So, don't go catching up on what you've missed during a fast, because studies have shown that that doesn't help. You lose weight because you eat less and not because you eat within a specific time constraint.

So, everyone needs to decide for themselves whether intermittent fasting (IF) or time-restricted eating (TRE) will add anything to their quality of life. Also, know that the benefits of

IF and TRE have more to do with your health and less to do with losing weight. Think about it before you begin. Read Professor Hanno Pijl's contribution to this book first.
Why should you want to try intermittent fasting? Make sure you are doing it for the right reasons. If "losing weight quickly" is the only reason, don't do it. If you do decide to do it, do it based on a conscious choice to improve your health. If you use the right approach and feel good about doing it, it can be a powerful method.

My personal advice: don't make the mistake I did, take it one step at a time. Start by eating moderately low-carb. If that feels good and you want to take things a step further because you're not losing weight, for instance, you can consider a keto cure or IF or TRE, or a combination of both. Read about it and ease into it gradually. Don't start going full keto or intermittent fasting straight away—even I don't do that! It may all sound very promising and trendy, but the main question is: how beneficial is it for you? Always put your health first, be realistic and respect your body. The most important question is: how does it feel for you? If it doesn't feel right, stop doing it!

Important note

Intermittent fasting is not recommended for people who are susceptible to eating disorders, pregnant women, the elderly, people with thyroid conditions, diabetes patients, people taking medication and underweight people. If you really do want to fast, be smart and do so only under professional guidance.

How do I transition from keto to low carb?

Once you've lost weight after following a ketogenic diet and you go back to eating as you did before, the pounds will start piling on again, which makes perfect sense to me. It's those poor eating habits that caused you to become overweight in the first place, so why wouldn't they do the same this time? Moreover, some people think they can reverse the damage they've created over decades with a 14-day keto cure. That's not how it works. The goal is to start changing the way you eat. A ketogenic diet can be an enlightening experience. See it as a way of gaining insight into how your body reacts and taking what you've learned with you. If you then switch to a moderately low-carb way of eating, I can guarantee that the weight will stay off. But make the transition smooth and gradual. You can incorporate many of your favorite keto dishes into your new lifestyle. If you're sensitive to carbs, schedule a few more keto days. Find your own rhythm, your own cycling balance.

How much fat should I eat after a keto diet?

Fat and carbs act like communicating vessels

When you switch from keto to a moderately low-carb diet, you'll start to eat slightly more carbs. This means that you'll be eating more fruit and starchy vegetables such as pumpkins, celeriac, beans or chickpeas. As you increase your intake of one thing, carbs in this case, you need to reduce your intake of something else, and in this case, that's fat. Consider fat and carbs as communicating vessels in your eating pattern. If you consume more of one, then you need to consume less of the other. But you need to make a choice.

Lots of (fast) carbs and lots of fat are a disastrous combination. In that respect, the traditional school of nutritional thought has it right: if you choose to eat plenty of carbs, you should eat very little fat. But the consequence is that people don't feel full, causing them to eat even more carbs. Moreover, those large quantities of carbs are highly addictive. That's why many people tend to function better with fewer carbs and more fat. The food tastes better, is more filling, and you end up with no more blood sugar peaks, no cravings, less hunger, more energy, fewer dips, more real food.

In nature, you rarely come across hyper-flavored foods that contain both plenty of carbs and plenty of fats. Carb- and fat-rich is the favored combination of the factory food industry: croissants, French fries, spice cakes, donuts, cookies, industrially produced sausages, chips, pizza ... It's the most fattening and unhealthy combination you can think of. Sadly enough, it's what forms the basis of our current eating culture, with all the common chronic diseases we're faced with as a result.

Women lose weight during a keto cure while men gain weight

This may sound like a caricature, but some people may recognize this phenomenon. The woman wants to lose a couple of pounds and follows a ketogenic diet; the man thinks it's all garbage and wants his potatoes whatever the cost. What does the woman do? She cooks recipes from the Keto Cure and prepares potatoes for her partner. Everyone is happy because the man finds to his surprise that the fat-rich food actually tastes really good. But she ends up losing weight while he starts to gain weight! Because he's eating food that's both high in carbs and fats. You can't have it both ways.

You need to make a choice. Either you eat plenty of carbs (like most vegans do) with less fat, or you eat fat-rich foods (as in a ketogenic or a moderately low-carb diet) with fewer carbs.

So, when you switch from a ketogenic diet to a moderately low-carb way of eating, go easy on the fat to compensate for the extra carbs you eat. It's not that carbs and fat don't go together; it's all about proportions: many (fast) carbs together with plenty of fat is not a good combination. There's nothing wrong with a breakfast with fruits and full-fat yogurt, but I wouldn't add sugar to the mix.

Tip

If you're following a ketogenic diet and in ketosis, but you're still gaining weight: reduce your fat intake.
If you're following a moderately low-carb diet and you're still gaining weight: try reducing your carb intake even further first.

Some more practical tips

I've a headache, lack energy, feel terrible, weak, dizzy, constipated ...

The famous "keto flu" is actually a group of symptoms that some people experience once they start a ketogenic diet. They could be withdrawal symptoms from reduced sugar intake, but generally these symptoms arise because of the reduced intake of salt. Ketosis stimulates the kidneys to secrete salt. That's why it's wise to drink more and eat slightly more salt, not only during the first few days but as long as you eat keto.

Many people who eat a carb-rich diet store too much salt and water; they have a swollen face or swollen feet. So when that salt leaves your body together with the moisture, that's actually a good thing—unless you secrete too much salt. This is often the root cause of many of these "keto flu" symptoms that we want to avoid. Because if you don't feel well, you won't be able to keep it up. The message here is to keep adding enough salt. Bear in mind that you'll often be doing your own cooking when you follow a keto diet. So you won't be eating industrially prepared foods, which often contain lots of salt. The salt now needs to come from what you add to your food. (Just to give an idea: 2 slices of bread contain 1 gram of salt).

The general daily recommendation is 6 grams of salt (= 2.4 g sodium) per day, which comes down to about 1 teaspoon of salt. According to Dr. Stephen Phinney, that level should be slightly higher: around 5 grams of sodium a day, especially when you're following a ketogenic diet. Salt is made up of 40% sodium and 60% chloride. So 12 grams of salt is good for 5 grams of sodium, which comes down to about 2 teaspoons of salt per day. Note that this advice is only for when you follow a keto diet and if you cook yourself. Prepared foods contain lots of salt, so if you add 2 teaspoonfuls of salt on top of that, you'll be taking in too much salt.

Besides salt, consuming enough magnesium, potassium, zinc, and iron is also essential. That's why it's essential to eat enough and a varied range of foods (such as the recipes in this book).

Please note!

Before you start increasing your salt intake, discuss this with your physician. Especially if you're being treated for high blood pressure or if you've a kidney or heart condition.

Tip: salty lemonade and broth

In the summer, I like to drink sparkling water with a little lemon juice and salt (fleur de sel). It's delicious. Or some delicious homemade broth in the winter. It's a great way to get those natural minerals inside you.

What should I drink during a keto cure?

It's wise to drink more when you're following a keto cure, because a ketogenic diet causes you to lose moisture. You can drink anything as long as it isn't sweetened—that includes sweeteners—and doesn't contain carbs. Homemade broth is ideal because it's also a rich source of minerals. As I said, a glass of sparkling water with a little salt and lemon juice is one of my favorite drinks. But coffee works as well, and apparently is even good for you, as long as you don't drink too much of it and it's unsweetened. Teas and herbal teas are good, healthy options—unsweetened, of course. I also like kombucha, but again, the same applies: the unsweetened version. Note that kombucha is a fermented drink, so sugars have been added to it, but living organisms digest these sugars during the fermentation process. The final product is a healthy, slightly sour drink full of beneficial nutrients that are also great for your gut bacteria. I've extensively discussed alcohol in my first *The Keto Cure* book. A glass of white wine or champagne is fine, as long as you can handle it.

How about snacks?

I recommend eating enough at mealtimes and avoiding snacks. Only eat in between meals if you're really hungry. Snacking throughout the day is a habit rather than a need, so try cutting it down. Always look at the bigger picture: if you're on track with your weight and you have guests over, a snack or appetizer once in a while won't hurt. It's about creating a balance and developing healthy habits. Eating in between meals is not a healthy habit.

How about having desserts while on a keto cure?

The idea that you can have the occasional dessert during a keto cure sounds appealing, and it makes it all manageable. This book contains several fun and delicious desserts. But I'd like to point out that you can't lose sight of your goal. These desserts are keto proof, but they're also very rich. If you eat too many of them, you won't lose weight. Everyone needs to look at their own situation. If you want to lose weight and have trouble doing so, eating desserts is not the best option. If you are on track, the occasional dessert won't hurt.

YOUR BODY IS NOT YOUR ENEMY, AND WILLPOWER IS NOT YOUR FRIEND

Working on your health should always be fun

I want to make my message very clear: don't be blinded by what other people do, as trendy as it may sound. As far as your health is concerned, it's all about listening to your body, staying true to yourself and not losing yourself in all that sweet talk. Everything looks easy on paper, and the question is: where do you begin?
Well, start where you are now. Ask yourself the following questions: what do I want, what is feasible for me and what makes me feel good? Think baby steps. I don't believe people when they say: I'm going to turn my life around starting on 1 January—you know, all those New Year's resolutions. You're only kidding yourself. Be honest with yourself. If you want to eat healthier, start now and don't wait until January.
Know that there are many ways that you can start eating healthier. The first step is to consume less prefab food and start eating more real food, as described in my book *Echt Eten* ('Real Food'). Cut back on sweet snacks. Eat less refined bread. Try eating fruit for breakfast. Adjust your eating habits using baby steps. See it as a journey of discovery, but one that should always be fascinating and fun. And know that it's not the end of the world when you revert to junk food once in a while; it's not even that bad. We're strong, and we can take it. But don't fight your body; your body is not the enemy, and willpower is not your friend. Your body and your mind make up one whole. Feel what goes on in your body. Make peace with it, love it, listen to it. You'll immediately notice the peace of mind this brings. And it will allow you to make better choices.
Eating healthy is not something you do for 14 days; it's a way of life. It's a choice, and that choice is choosing for yourself. So don't let yourself be led or misled by others. If a ketogenic diet doesn't feel right for you, don't do it. There are plenty of other ways to eat healthily. If intermittent fasting doesn't feel right after reading the chapter about it, don't do it. Start with low-carb, and your journey will light the way. The important part is getting started. And whatever you do, it should be fun and exciting.

I DO EVERYTHING THE WAY I SHOULD, BUT I'M NOT LOSING WEIGHT!

That's a frustrating situation to be in, especially when you have people around you who are losing weight. But not everyone reacts to keto the same way. The more insulin-resistant you are, the harder it is to reach ketosis. Are you overweight? Take a good look at what you eat on any given day. How much do you eat? Eating too little can be just as big of a problem as overeating.
Are you in ketosis? Check this first; you can use test strips to do this quickly and easily (see *The Keto Cure*). I'm not a proponent of keeping track of macros, but if you're not losing weight and you want to know why, this could be a good way to find out.

Are you not reaching ketosis? > You're eating too many carbs for your body/activity level. Concentrate on reducing your carb intake even further. Are you really following the book, or are you eating more? By snacking, for example? Are you eating too many nuts? Nuts are good for you, but they contain quite a few carbs, so don't eat too many of them. What else contains carbs? Learn which vegetables have plenty of carbs. The results may surprise you. Regularly check a carb chart or carb counter; they are readily available online.
What to do: Eat fewer carbs, but don't reduce your fat intake.

Are you in ketosis, but you're not losing weight? > You're eating too much for your body/activity level. We don't restrict calorie intake during a ketogenic diet, but that doesn't mean calories don't play any role at all. If you overeat, you won't lose weight. Read the article on "How much fat am I allowed to eat while following a ketogenic diet?" (see page 21)
What to do: Eat less fat.

Perhaps you're not eating enough? > You want to lose weight quickly, so you're eating less. You're probably feeling hungry too. The idea that "the less I eat, the more weight I'll lose" is not a good starting point. Because then you're essentially reducing your calorie intake, forcing your body to go into hibernation mode. Read the section titled "Eating keto means dieting through eating". Satisfaction plays a key role. (See page 12.) Check what you eat on any given day and calculate your calorie intake if necessary to check whether you're eating enough.
What to do: Increase your fat intake.

Are you constantly hungry? > You're not eating enough protein and fats. If you're constantly hungry, you won't be able to keep this up for long. Going hungry doesn't mean that you're going to lose weight, on the contrary! The art lies in consuming just enough fats and proteins to keep you from feeling hungry and to turn your body into an efficient fat burner. Proteins fill the most, followed by fats. So eat slightly more proteins and fats. Do this gradually, one step at a time, and observe what happens before taking the next step.
What to do: Increase your protein and your fat intake.

Are you not hungry, and you're not eating too many carbs? > You're basically on the right track. But maybe you need to take it one step further: consider time-restricted eating. Skip breakfast, for example. If this fits within your lifestyle and you use the right approach, it can make all the difference. Read more about time-restricted eating on page 46.
What to do: Consider time-restricted eating or intermittent fasting.

Perhaps you're not overweight? > Your body could be at the right weight. It's your body and not you that decides how much weight you're supposed to lose. We've a habit of saying: just 3 or 5 more pounds. But what you want doesn't count; your body decides when you're in balance. We're not all born to go through life a size 6. Respect your body. Losing weight is not the primary goal; improving your health is. Also, know that losing weight is not a linear process. Enjoy the delicious food.
What to do: Eat healthily, stick to it, and let your body do the rest.

Eating is not only about health or what you put in your mouth. It's also about savoring the moment, spending time with friends, romance, being creative, and connecting with others. Whatever way of eating you choose, keep it fun and enjoyable, not only for yourself but also for others. If eating is getting you down, you're on the wrong track.

*Eating is so much more than just feeding your body.
It's about savoring the moment and creating the
perfect setting for those special moments.*

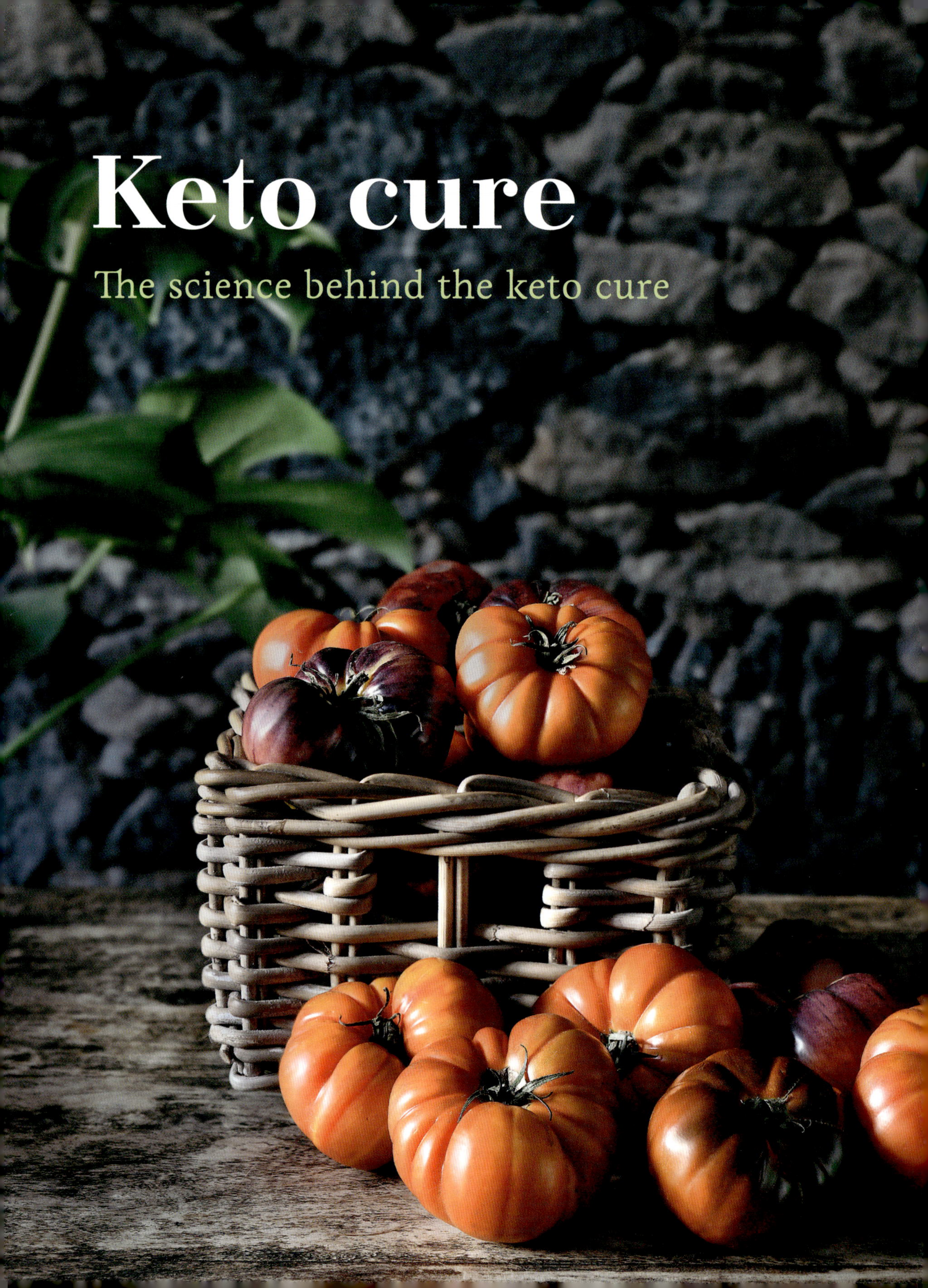

Keto cure

The science behind the keto cure

© Marco Okhuizen

Prof. dr. Hanno Pijl

Intermittent fasting and time-restricted eating

Intermittent fasting

We've known for about 80 years that limiting food increases the lifespan of rats under laboratory conditions. Give them 30% less than the control group (who are given as much as they want), and they clearly not only age more slowly, but they remain healthier as they do so. For example, cancer is far less prevalent among the animals who were given less to eat.
Why is that? And does limiting food intake have a similar effect on people? And even if it does work, always eating less than you actually want is an enormous challenge, particularly in a society that constantly tempts us to consume food. Is periodically fasting a more feasible alternative? And does it matter when you eat? Those are the questions that we'll try to answer in this book.

Why eating makes us age

There have been hundreds, if not thousands, of studies with a variety of animal species (from worms to mice and apes) that all show similar results: eating less than "normal" in the lab increases lifespan and reduces the chance of (chronic) diseases. Ageing and chronic disease result from damaged cells and tissues. So how does eating less than normal under laboratory conditions lead to reduced cell damage?

Firstly, it's important to define what we mean by "normal" in this context. Animals in the lab generally are given more than enough food. They eat until they're full, and sometimes more (just like people who are offered food they like). There are scientists who suggest that restricting food in captivity actually prevents the harmful effects caused by overeating. But why is overeating bad? The initial logical thought is that overeating leads to being overweight, and we all know that being overweight is not healthy. But there's more to it than that.

When we eat something, it's nearly always followed by an inflammatory response in the body. That response is necessary to repair the damage caused by our metabolism processing the food. Processing food costs energy. When the power plants in our cells, the mitochondria,

generate energy, they release what are known as free radicals. These free radicals are toxic. When produced in large quantities, they damage the cells in our bodies. That damage provokes a reaction from the immune system: an inflammation occurs, which is meant to repair the damage. Once the damage has been repaired, the inflammation quickly goes away.
So, the short-term immune system response to food is a very natural and essentially beneficial response. However, when we constantly ingest food (as is the case with lab animals who are given more than enough food—and people in our current society), this inflammatory response is never given a rest. The result is chronic inflammation. When inflammation becomes chronic, that can lead to further damage to cells rather than repairing cells. So eating too often can have harmful effects.

Eating too much is also harmful, on the one hand because of a more intense inflammatory response after a meal, and on the other hand because it leads to becoming overweight. When we eat more than our bodies need, we store the extra energy as fat tissue. There are three important fat stores in the body: under the skin of the bottom and thighs, under the skin of the abdomen, and in the abdominal cavity (between the intestines, liver and other intestinal organs). When fat cells (especially those in the abdominal cavity) grow, they become inflamed for what are still unknown reasons. As long as those too-large fat cells remain in the abdomen, the inflammation persists. This chronic inflammation is seen as an important cause for almost all diseases that are more common with overweight (such as type 2 diabetes, cardiovascular disease, cancer and asthma).

As I mentioned earlier, ageing and illness is a result of damaged cells and cell tissue. The ageing process is partly driven by the cell damage incurred as a by-product of our metabolism. Eating too much and too often, but also eating the wrong types of food, plays an important role. Going into detail about food quality and health here is taking it too far. But eating a varied diet and as little processed food as possible (as is the case in all the recipes in this book) are crucial rules. However, it should now be clear why eating less slows down the ageing process and reduces the chance of disease. Yet eating less is very difficult in an environment where food is readily available. *Temporarily* eating less requires a lot less willpower. The question that remains is: do intermittent fasting and/or time-restricted eating also have a positive effect on your health?

Fasting from an evolutionary perspective

Let me first dive into our evolutionary history to illustrate why we tend to eat everything that's put in front of us and what fasting does to our bodies.

Humans diverged genetically from apes some six million years ago. Since then we've evolved as hunter-gatherers into what we are today. Every day, we had to go out in search of food, the availability of which varied significantly. Periods of food scarcity were frequent, and our physiology adapted to survive those periods. Evolution has given us plenty of protective mechanisms that prevent and repair the damage caused by lack of food (and the lack of energy and building materials for our bodies). After all, a lack of energy and nutrients can prove fatal in a relatively short time, and everything needs to be done to survive these periods of food scarcity. People can survive up to 60 days without food (but not without water). On the other hand, we developed the (genetically determined!) characteristic that drove us to eat as much food as possible when it was available. We stored the surplus food as fat to keep in reserve for when food was scarce again. However, our physiology is not adapted to overeating. We were hardly ever too heavy or fat, because there was hardly ever more than enough food to eat. And the consequences of overeating are not potentially lethal in the short term, but only in the long term. So, nature hasn't protected us from the effects of being overweight.

Fasting: what happens to our bodies?

The effects of fasting on our physiology are highly diverse and very powerful, with the aim of surviving frequent periods of food scarcity as healthily as possible; it's a process that has been developed over millions of years of evolution. What exactly happens in our bodies when we fast?

Fat burning and ketones

Glucose and fatty acids are our most important fuel sources. We have relatively little storage capacity for glucose. Any surplus energy is mostly stored as fat. So, when we fast, we quickly switch to fat instead of glucose as our most important fuel source. When we burn a lot of fat, ketones are produced in the liver as a by-product of this process. We go into mild ketosis, the same ketosis we have when we eat few carbs (and also use our glucose stocks sparingly). The ketones act as an alternative fuel source for almost all our tissues, but also impact on the functioning of our cells. They help ensure that the processes described below are activated.

"Sensing" fuels and building materials

Like all other animals, humans have a highly complex physiological system that can "sense" how much fuel and building materials are available. The fact that we feel full when we've eaten enough is concrete proof of this process. But a lot more goes on than you think. All our cells have sensors that register how many amino acids (building blocks) and glucose or fatty acids (fuel) are consumed. If there are enough, cells will start to grow and multiply. When we fast, very little comes in and the cell adjusts its metabolism accordingly in various ways. Ketones also play a role in this process. Moreover, endocrine systems that coordinate the physiological response by sending signals to tissues are activated or deactivated. For instance, the concentration of insulin and the insulin-like growth factor (IGF) in the blood becomes very low. Those are powerful growing agents that are deactivated when no fuel or building materials are available.

Autophagy

When we take in too little fuel, our bodies initially cut back on energy use; energy is no longer used for cell growth and multiplication, but for cell maintenance and repair. A process is activated that converts damaged and unusable cell material into fuel or recycles the material as building materials: autophagy. As explained earlier, all our cells become damaged over time. Damaged cell structures are removed during the autophagy process. As long as we've enough food on board, the cells will focus on growth and multiplication and far less on maintenance. Autophagy is then largely dormant. When we eat less than we need for cell growth and multiplication, autophagy becomes a fuel source. At the same time, autophagy causes the cells to clean themselves up.

Hormesis

When a nutrition shortage is imminent, the cells arm themselves against stress. The general biological principle involved in this process is called "hormesis". More than a century ago, the German pharmacologist Hugo Schulz described how a large dose of formic acid could encourage the growth of yeast cells, while a high dose of that same substance killed the yeast cells. He initially thought this was due to a mistake in how the experiment was conducted, but repeated experiments kept showing the same results. He expanded his experiments to test other disinfecting substances that were commonly used in surgery and the results were exactly the same. Over the course of the past century, his findings were confirmed through other studies, leading to a universally applicable biological principle: mild stress (in any form) triggers protective mechanisms to counter all other forms of stress. So an imminent shortage of fuel and building blocks when we eat little or nothing not only leads to processes that protect us from that shortage, but also from hazardous substances and radioactive and solar radiation. Moreover, the mild stress resulting from short-term fasting protects cells from the damage that our metabolism causes through the release of free radicals, as described earlier. But the natural law always applies that the intense stress of long-term fasting will eventually prove fatal. We don't yet know how long fasting can continue before it becomes hazardous to your health.

Calories or specific nutrients?

Are the hormonal changes, autophagy and hormesis during fasting caused by a lack of calories or is it about specific nutrients? Less glucose and fewer proteins seem to be the main triggers. That makes sense when you remember that glucose is our most important fuel and protein our most important source for our bodies' building blocks. When these essential nutrients are in short supply, the body has to switch gears. Food with very little glucose and protein has almost the same effect on our physiology as full fasting. Valter Longo, a biologist and professor on ageing from Los Angeles, suggested that periodic fasting could be made easier with a diet consisting of no sugars and very little protein, and only fiber-rich carbs from vegetables and healthy fats (700-100 kcal/day, ⅓ of what you normally eat in a day). We call that "modified fasting".

The ketogenic diet and autophagy/hormesis

Insufficient studies have been conducted so far to be certain of the effects of ketogenic nutrition on autophagy and hormesis. There are a couple of studies conducted on rats and mice that report the activation of autophagy with ketogenic nutrition, but I believe this is not enough to be conclusive. There are also indications that ketones play a role in hormesis. They activate genes that are associated with the protection of cells against the hazardous effects of free radicals. It also makes sense that ketogenic nutrition activates autophagy and hormeses; we take in very little glucose, our most important fuel source. That is most probably experienced as a mild form of stress, which in turn activates autophagy and hormesis during a ketogenic diet. Ketogenic nutrition, however, also often contains substantial quantities of protein. A temporary restriction in protein, but also perhaps a decrease in the total number of calories consumed, will probably intensify autophagy and hormesis during ketogenic nutrition. Valter Longo's diet is, in fact, one of those ketogenic diets with very little protein. He calls it "fasting mimicking", because the physiological effects are practically identical to those associated with full fasting.

The ketogenic diet and disease

A recent review of the health effects of ketogenic nutrition states that "there is reason for optimism, but further research is required." I fully agree with this conclusion. We know from research conducted with mice that a ketogenic diet reduces diabetes, particularly in mice with obesity and metabolic syndrome. There are further indications that a ketogenic diet also reduces the risks of neurodegenerative diseases (such as Parkinson's disease and dementia) and maybe even cancer, particularly with mice with metabolic syndrome. Ketogenic nutrition leads to quick improvement in glucose metabolism in people with (type 2) diabetes. Very little research has been carried out into the long-term effects of ketogenic nutrition.

Effects on health

It is, therefore, perfectly imaginable that autophagy and hormesis can play a contributing factor in disease prevention and slowing down the ageing process. Autophagy keeps the cells clean and healthy on the one hand, while hormesis keeps more damage from occurring on the other hand. But it also goes without saying that you shouldn't fast for too long. At the end of the day, a lack of fuel and building blocks will prove fatal. So, is intermittent (= with breaks in between) fasting beneficial to your health?

Intermittent fasting: is it healthy?

You can try intermittent fasting in several ways. Most studies focus on 1) fully fasting every other day; 2) eating nothing or less than 600 calories per day for two consecutive days of the week; 3) "modified" fasting for five consecutive days every month; or 4) time-restricted eating, where you consume everything you eat in one day in a timespan of eight hours, for example. You fast during the remaining 16 hours of the day ("16:8 fasting"). Time-restricted eating works differently from intermittent fasting, so we will treat this separately.

So far, most research conducted on the effects of intermittent fasting and time-restricted eating on health has been carried out with animals. The general assumption, however, is that these effects will largely also apply to humans, because the biochemical adjustments involved with fasting were the same in all the animals studied; mice in particular are very similar to humans in terms of their metabolism. Nonetheless, it's important to establish whether (intermittent) fasting has the same health benefits for humans as it does for animals. In recent years, increasing research using human subjects has suggested that this is indeed the case.

Chronic disease

Animals that take part in intermittent fasting are healthier and less prone to damaged cells and disease than animals who are allowed to eat what they want whenever they want. Although the extent of the effect varies somewhat between the various regimes and different animal species, a clear pattern emerges. Intermittent fasting reduces inflammation, mitigates cell damage, protects against stress, improves brain function, lowers blood pressure and improves cholesterol levels. This applies to almost all the animal species that were involved in the studies (from worms to mice and apes). Intermittent fasting in mice reduces the risk of diabetes and cancer. In addition, there are strong indications that it also reduces the risks of developing auto-immune diseases (such as multiple sclerosis and arthritis) and neurodegenerative conditions (including Parkinson's disease and dementia).

Intermittent fasting seems to have similar effects on humans. It reduces inflammation, improves metabolism, and lowers blood pressure, cholesterol levels and all sorts of growth factors. Although no research has been conducted into this as of yet, it could potentially decrease the risk of chronic diseases such as diabetes, cardiovascular disease, cancer, asthma and arthritis.

Weight loss

The effect on body mass varies and is primarily dependent on how strict the fast is and the initial body weight. Most overweight people who participate in intermittent fasting lose weight. People with a normal weight often don't.

The effects on health can only partly be accounted for by weight loss. The mechanisms described earlier (ketosis, autophagy, hormesis) play an essential role.

Which form of intermittent fasting is most effective?

For humans, we're still not sure which form of intermittent fasting is most effective. To begin with, we don't know exactly how long you need to fast before achieving optimal activation of the protective mechanisms in your body (autophagy and hormesis). Moreover, everyone reacts differently to food and fasting. We do know that the keto acid production starts to increase after an average of 12 hours of fasting. But keto acid production really gets under way after 48 hours. If you want to optimally activate the protective mechanisms, then you'll probably have to fast for at least 48 hours. However, not everyone reacts well to fasting for so long. It's a matter of trying out which form of intermittent fasting works best for you.

Modified fasting

As I mentioned earlier, the effects of fasting are mostly the result of an (imminent) shortage of glucose and protein. So you can achieve the same results with nutrition that contains hardly any sugars or starches (our nutritional source of glucose) and very little protein (less than 25 grams per day). You are allowed to eat some complex, fiber-rich, indigestible carbs from green vegetables and healthy fats. The number of calories can best be limited to less than 1000 per day. That makes fasting more difficult for some people. This diet is highly ketogenic. But it contains far less protein and calories than the ketogenic diet described in this book, and is therefore only suitable for short stretches at a time (a couple of days).

It's not easy to plan your own meals in this way. The closest guideline is to eat only vegetables (but not root vegetables), for example in soups. Vegetables contain primarily complex carbs and water (and lots of vitamins and minerals), and little protein, fat and calories. You can eat as much as you want and still have a hard time exceeding the 1000-calorie daily limit. I sometimes advise a "vegetable fast" to my patients, and I do this once every six to eight weeks for a period of four to five days.

Safety

Fasting is generally very safe if you're healthy. People can fast for days without any detrimental effects. But there are limits. Firstly to the length of the fasting period. We would never recommend that anyone does a full fast for more than ten days. And being in good condition to start with is essential. Make sure you've consumed enough nutrients before starting your fast. Eat healthy (unprocessed, varied foods). And keep drinking enough water, coffee and unsweetened tea! During the first couple of days, you'll lose mostly water and salt.

Side effects

Some people experience dizziness (especially when getting up) and listlessness after a couple of days, sometimes even earlier. A little extra salt might help in this case. Headaches and nausea can also occur. These symptoms disappear almost immediately as soon as you start to eat again.

Fasting during illness

Never fast when you're suffering from a condition without consulting your physician first! Your medication (for example blood pressure or glucose metabolism medications) often need to be adjusted accordingly. If you're suffering from other conditions, always start small, for example by fasting just one day, and don't do a full fast but stick to "modified" fasting (see previous).

Time-restricted eating

Time-restricted eating refers to eating everything you would eat in any given day within a certain timeframe. This can be in an eight-hour timespan, for example between 12:00 and 20:00 or between 08:00 and 16:00. The rest of those 24 hours you're limited to water, coffee and unsweetened tea. So, you essentially fast for 16 hours a day. That's why this eating pattern is also sometimes referred to as intermittent fasting. Decreasing your food intake, however, is only partly responsible for the effects; they mostly have to do with respecting your biological clock.

The biological clock

Back in the day, we used to live according to the rhythm of the day. We were active as soon as the sun was up and we went to sleep when it got dark. We only ate during the day. And all that in a highly regular cycle. Our physiology adjusted to this rhythm. All our metabolic processes are geared towards being active and eating during the daytime and sleeping and fasting at night. Our brains coordinate those processes via a highly complex physiological system called our biological clock. This clock has a rhythm that's in sync with the natural daily rhythm. The clock's timing is adjusted when light enters our eyes and when we eat. If that happens outside of the natural daylight period, the clock is disrupted, and many processes in our bodies no longer function in sync with each other. And that's exactly what we do in today's society.

Biological clock disruption and disease

Today, our activities—including our eating activities—are almost entirely independent from this daily rhythm. As soon as food is consumed, it's registered by the endocrine system and the sensors I described earlier. Those systems are in direct contact with the biological clock, which adjusts the metabolism accordingly. When that occurs in agreement with your clock's natural rhythm, the food is processed optimally. However, most people eat throughout the day. Moreover, we tend to consume most of our calories after sundown. That doesn't agree with the natural rhythm of your body clock at all, and so the metabolism is disrupted, increasing the risk of developing conditions and diseases. Diabetes, cardiovascular disease, but also cancer and asthma are more common among people who work in shifts. And that relationship is independent of other lifestyle factors. But the clock is also disrupted by adjustments to the waking and sleeping routine on the weekends (people go to bed later and sleep longer in the mornings, but also eat at different times than they do during the week). It's likely that this also increases the risk factor.

Time-restricted eating "resets" the biological clock

By consuming all your food regularly in a certain timeframe during the day, you're "resetting" your biological clock, to a certain extent, to its natural rhythm, especially when the consumption takes place during daylight hours. It allows the metabolism to recover and reduces the risk of disease. I have underlined the word regularly, because this is essential to achieving the desired effect. As soon as you change the rhythm of your meals, the clock is disrupted again. Timing is also crucial. Because the day starts in the morning, it may seem logical to eat your first meal in the morning. There are indications that eating everything within an 8:00 to 16:00 timeframe is more effective than in a 12:00 to 20:00 timeframe. But the latter is still much better than grazing throughout the day (and evening). And eating between 8:00 and 16:00 is not an option for almost anyone living in the current social context.

“As opposed to eating whatever you want whenever you want, time-restricted eating reduces inflammation, improves blood glucose levels and fat metabolism rates and lowers blood pressure, regardless of body weight. It reduces the risk of diabetes and cardiovascular conditions, and there are indications that it reduces the risk of certain types of cancer.”

Hanno Pijl

ENDOCRINOLOGIST, PROFESSOR OF DIABETOLOGY
AT THE LEIDEN UNIVERSITY MEDICAL CENTER, THE NETHERLANDS

Time-restricted eating and health

Most of our information on the effects of time-restricted eating on health comes from animal experiments. As opposed to eating whatever you want whenever you want, time-restricted eating reduces inflammation, improves blood glucose levels and fat metabolism rates and lowers blood pressure, regardless of body weight. It reduces the risk of diabetes and cardiovascular conditions, and there are some indications that it reduces the risk of certain types of cancer. Time-restricted eating often lowers body weight, but the degree in which weight loss takes place is dependent on the animals’ initial weight. Obese mice that previously “grazed” night and day tend to lose much more weight than those who start out at a normal weight.

Only short-term studies have been conducted with human subjects so far (mostly up to twelve weeks) with people who are slightly or very overweight. Most studies restrict food intake to a timeframe of eight to ten hours a day. The first meal is usually consumed between 10:00 and 12:00 and the last meal is consumed eight to ten hours later. These studies have shown an improvement in metabolism.
The glucose levels and the fat profiles in the blood, as well as blood pressure levels improve. This will most probably decrease the risk of diseases such as diabetes and cardiovascular disease. The weight always lowers a little bit (a few kilograms after 12 to 16 weeks), particularly with people who are overweight.
No studies have been carried out into the long-term effects of time-restricted eating.

Time-restricted eating is not intermittent fasting

Although time-restricted eating often (but not always) leads to a reduced food intake, that's not the only cause of the health benefits associated with it.
Mice that are allowed to freely eat fat and sugar-rich foods and eat throughout the day and night will become overweight and develop diabetes without exception. When you give these mice the same quantities of food, but you only offer them food during the night (mice are nocturnal animals) then they will eat the exact same amount, but they grow much less fat and they stay healthy! Calorie restriction contributes to improved health, but because that's not the only mechanism involved, I believe that time-restricted eating is something different from intermittent fasting.

Time-restricted eating, how do you do that?

Time-restricted eating is relatively simple. You choose a timeframe within the day when you can eat anything you want. As I've mentioned earlier, an early timeframe from 08:00 to 16:00 is probably the most effective (although this hasn't been confirmed yet). This is, however, not manageable for most people because of social restrictions. In that case, a timeframe of 12:00 to 20:00 would be a good alternative. Don't make it any later. The more you eat outside of your natural diurnal rhythm, the fewer the health benefits. From 20:00 to 12:00, you only drink water, coffee and unsweetened tea. Try to stick to your choice of timeframe as much as possible. If you change around too much, your biological clock is thrown out of kilter and that may affect your health.

Safety

Time-restricted eating is safe for everyone and doesn't have any side effects, normally speaking. I hear from some people that they really can't make it through the morning without food.
I would say: choose the timeframe that works best for you. It's also a matter of getting used to it. People who are sick should consult a physician before they start time-restricted eating, although there are hardly any negative side effects to this approach. But the dosage of your blood pressure or glucose metabolism medication may need to be adjusted to prevent dips in glucose and blood pressure levels.

© Roos Mestdagh

Dr. William Cortvriendt

The ketogenic diet and misconceptions about cholesterol

When I talk to dieticians and physicians about the ketogenic diet, I often hear comments like the following: "It's a diet with an awful lot of fat," or "That can't be healthy." Usually followed by a comment that such a diet increases cholesterol levels in the blood leading to an increased risk of cardiovascular disease.
They're right in saying that the ketogenic diet contains a lot of fat—70 to 75 percent even—including plenty of saturated fats. And these fats increase the cholesterol level in the blood. In that respect, those comments are completely correct. However, the premise that so many fats and a raised cholesterol level are by definition unhealthy is not. Consuming plenty of fat is actually very healthy, as long as they're the right fats. And a high cholesterol level doesn't have to be unhealthy, especially when it's the result of a ketogenic diet. In short, it's time to set some things straight about healthy and unhealthy fats and the cholesterol phenomenon.

Concerns about increasing heart attack rates

Over the course of many millions of years of evolution, our genes have always been able to adapt to what were usually slowly-changing environmental factors. Over the last century, however, the amount of carbs in our diet has skyrocketed, most notably as a component of industrially processed foods, sodas and juices. Increasing quantities of sugar and industrial trans fats were used to flavor these processed foods. Trans fats in particular were used because these fats don't go rancid like their natural counterparts and increase the shelf life of a product. Our genes haven't had enough time to adjust to these kinds of changes.

Because of a rapid increase in the number of fatal heart attacks, governments in western countries became increasingly concerned about what their citizens ate after the Second World War. The suspicion had arisen that the fats and cholesterol in our food were the cause of cardiovascular disease. They noticed that every time a patient died from a heart attack and the blood vessels were inspected, it turned out that these were clogged up because the blood vessel lining

was filled with fats and cholesterol. So the inevitable conclusion was that these components in our nutrition were the culprits.
It was around the same time that the world-famous American nutrition expert Ancel Keys came up with the idea of seeing if there was a correlation between fat consumption in different countries and the number of fatal heart attacks. He hypothesized that fatal heart attacks would be more prevalent in countries with the highest fat consumption. Keys passionately devoted most of his career to finding proof to support his hypothesis. The published results became known as the so-called "Seven Countries Study", in which he illustrated the correlation between the consumption of mainly saturated fats and cholesterol levels in the blood in certain countries on the one hand, and on the other hand the number of deaths related to cardiovascular disease. This study was later highly criticized for a number of reasons. First of all, the original study did not contain 7 countries but 21 countries—14 countries had been removed from the study because their findings did not agree with the hypothesis that fats and cholesterol were responsible for cardiovascular disease. In fact, later studies revealed that there wasn't a single correlation between the number of deaths caused by heart failure and fat consumption, but that there was a correlation between heart failure and the consumption of sugar, cake and other baked goods containing high carbohydrate levels.

Government nutritional guidelines from 1977 onwards and their consequences

Despite the fact that, in hindsight, Keys' conclusions were incorrect, they were adopted across the globe by governments, physicians, dieticians and even the WHO. In the US in 1977, there was even a formal directive from what was then called the McGovern senate committee to restrict the consumption of fats and replace fats with carbohydrates with the aim of reducing the risk of cardiovascular disease. This advice led to a rapid increase in the consumption of carbohydrates and a decrease in what had become relatively expensive fruits and vegetables. And the food industry immediately followed suit by stocking supermarket shelves with industrially processed food filled with sugars and other carbs. Natural fats and cholesterol were removed from foods wherever possible and partially replaced by linoleic acid, a so-called polyunsaturated fat that was supposed to be good for the heart and blood vessels. We were introduced to new terms such as "cholesterol-free", "reduced-fat", "fat-free", "skimmed", and "light".
The desired result, a decrease in the number of heart attacks, however, was not achieved with the guidelines offered by the McGovern senate commission, not even when the desired lower cholesterol levels in the blood were detected. What did happen was that, immediately after the publication of this advice, in the US, overweight, obesity, and a few years later type 2 diabetes, started their irrevocable increase, later followed by an increase in cardiovascular disease and cancer. And wherever in the world the same guidelines were followed—including the Netherlands and Belgium—the same trends arose as in the US.

Meanwhile, studies were showing that populations that ate extremely large quantities of fats, such as the Maasai in Kenya, the Samburu in Uganda, the Inuit in Alaska and the Polynesians on the Tokelau islands had almost no instance of cardiovascular disease, and no records of conditions such as obesity and diabetes. Ever since the diet of the people of the Tokelau islands in Polynesia, that had consisted mostly of fish and coconuts, was replaced by low-fat, carb-rich "healthy" western nutrition imported from New Zealand, the residents of this island group have been among the unhealthiest people on Earth. Obesity, type 2 diabetes, and heart failure have become the standard among this population group. Despite the disastrous results of the McGovern nutritional guidelines, low-fat and carb-rich foods are still being promoted as healthy foods by many governments and therefore also the food industry. Thankfully, this view is changing, and increasing numbers of foods that contain natural fats are being recommended by the Dutch and Belgian governments.

What we know now about healthy and unhealthy fats

Gradually we are also now seeing a consensus arise about what the healthy and unhealthy fats are. First of all, the industrial trans fats we mentioned earlier, which are mostly found in solid margarines and baked goods, are extremely unhealthy. Thankfully, these fats have mostly been phased out of processed foods.
And we've let go of the idea that all so-called polyunsaturated fats are supposed to be healthy. This does apply to the omega-3 fatty acids from this group that are mostly found in fatty fish and nuts. But it certainly doesn't apply to the omega-6 fatty acids, of which linoleic acid is the most common, that induces inflammation and of which we ingest far too much, particularly through industrially processed foods. The linoleic acid that until recently had been abundantly added to margarines to lower cholesterol levels and improve people's cardiovascular health no longer appears on TV ads. There are indications that linoleic acid does exactly the opposite and is responsible for more heart attacks. Moreover, linoleic acid is a contributing factor to converting harmless cholesterol into unhealthy cholesterol.[5]

Not to mention that heating the linoleic acid present in plant-based oils and butters causes this polyunsaturated fatty acid to oxidize, increasing the conversion process from healthy to unhealthy cholesterol (see below).
Opinion is also gradually shifting with regards to saturated fatty acids that increase cholesterol levels (which they do).[6]

5 Ramsden C. Zamora D. Leelarthaepin B. et al. Use of dietary linoleic acid for secondary prevention of coronary heart disease and death: evaluation of recovered data from the Sydney Diet Heart Study and updated meta-analyses. *BMJ*. 2013 ; 346 : e8707.

6 Astrup A. Magkos F. Bier D. et al. Saturated Fats and Health: A Reassessment and Proposal for Food-Based Recommendations. JACC State-of-the-Art Review. *J Am Coll Cardiol*. 2020: 76(7), 844–857.

Studies have repeatedly shown that the consumption of these fats doesn't increase the prevalence of cardiovascular disease.[6] In fact, the opposite seems to be the case: there are plenty of indications that suggest the more you replace carbohydrates with saturated fats, the lower your risk of having a heart attack.

Confusion about cholesterol

The scientific field has been sending apparently conflicting messages about cholesterol and cardiovascular disease:

- Cholesterol plays a role in cardiovascular disease.
- High cholesterol levels are seen as a risk factor for cardiovascular disease and should be treated with medication to lower cholesterol levels (statins).
- Consuming more polyunsaturated fats lowers cholesterol levels in the blood. Consuming more saturated fats increases cholesterol levels. That's why unsaturated fats are often considered healthy and saturated fats are seen as unhealthy.
- But the consumption of more saturated fats does not lead to an increase in the occurrence of heart attacks, despite the higher cholesterol levels! In fact, as we've mentioned earlier, replacing some of the carbohydrates in our diet with saturated fats leads to a reduction in the number of heart attacks!
- If we lower cholesterol levels with medications such as statins, the number of heart attacks and the resulting mortality rate does go down.

To understand why lowering cholesterol levels by consuming fewer saturated fats doesn't lead to fewer heart attacks, but the use of statins does, we need to know more about cholesterol itself, one of the most essential substances for our bodies.

What is cholesterol?

Cholesterol is one of the most important building blocks in our bodies; animal life would not be possible without cholesterol! Cholesterol is an essential building block for our cell walls and serves as raw material for the production of various substances in our bodies such as steroid hormones, bile, and vitamin D. But the most striking function of cholesterol is as a building block for our nervous system, including the brain. No less than 25 percent of all cholesterol in our bodies is located in the brain, and it seems that the more cholesterol is present in our cell walls, the better our brain is able to function. In contrast to prevailing opinion, very little of the cholesterol in our bodies comes from food, most of it's produced from smaller molecules in the liver. By far, most of the cholesterol in our food isn't absorbed; it passes through and is excreted from our bodies unchanged. And, when we do absorb some of the cholesterol from our food, the liver compensates for this by simply producing less cholesterol. The recent dietary guidelines on reducing cholesterol by eating fewer eggs, butter, shrimp and liver can be scrapped straight away! The main people who benefit from margarines that are purported to restrict the absorption of cholesterol from foods are the manufacturers themselves.

Yet, everyone knows that cholesterol levels in the blood are a highly important indicator for the risk of cardiovascular disease. However, it's not so much a matter of the total cholesterol levels, but mainly the proportion of "healthy" and "unhealthy" cholesterol. So how does that work?

Cholesterol levels in our blood

Almost everyone has grown up with the idea that cholesterol is harmful to your health and that high values in the blood lead to arteriosclerosis and eventually heart attacks and strokes. Until recently, physicians were told the exact same thing during their medical studies, and they're still being told this by visiting physicians who promote cholesterol-reducing medication. And if the cholesterol values in your blood are too high, then you immediately need to take in cholesterol-lowering statins, usually for the rest of your life. But there is a problem here. What if I told you that research has shown that higher cholesterol levels lead to improved cognitive performance, a better memory, an improved immune system, a reduced risk of inflammation and a reduced risk of cancer and Parkinson's disease? Moreover, studies among elderly people have shown that the higher your total cholesterol levels in your blood, the lower your mortality risk.[7]
So why would you want to lower cholesterol levels in your blood with statins, and how do they work? The reason is simple: your body contains both healthy and unhealthy cholesterol and the statins lower mostly the unhealthy cholesterol levels.

Good and bad cholesterol

Cholesterol is a fatty substance that is insoluble in water and therefore doesn't dissolve in the bloodstream. Still, cholesterol needs to be transported safely from the liver to various parts of the body without fatty globules forming in the bloodstream that could clog up blood vessels. Our bodies have solved this problem by surrounding the cholesterol in the bloodstream with molecules with a hydrophilic side that can be mixed with water and a lipophilic side with the fatty cholesterol. These molecules are also known as "lipoproteins". We currently know that cholesterol in the bloodstream is present either as a compound with plenty of lipoproteins, called *high-density lipoprotein* (HDL) cholesterol or as a compound with relatively few lipoproteins, known as the *low-density lipoprotein* (LDL) cholesterol.
The importance of HDL and LDL cholesterol, commonly referred to as "good" and "bad" cholesterol, is that HDL cholesterol is actually very good for the heart and blood vessels, and too much LDL cholesterol is not. The amount of HDL cholesterol matters a lot. So much so that the 20 percent of women with the lowest HDL cholesterol levels are three times more likely to

7 Weverling-Rijnsburger A. Blauw G. Lagaay A. et al. Total cholesterol and risk of mortality in the oldest old. Lancet. 1997; 350(9085): 1119-1123.
Takata Y. Ansai T. Soh I. et al. Serum total cholesterol concentration and 10-year mortality in an 85-year-old population. *Clin Interv Aging.* 2014; 13(9): 293-300.
De Lau L. Koudstaal P, Hofman A. et al. Serum cholesterol levels and the risk of Parkinson's disease. *Am J Epidemiol.* 2006; 164(10):998-1002.

8 Wilson P. Abbott R. Castelli W. High density lipoprotein cholesterol and mortality. The Framingham Heart Study. 1988; 8(6): 737-741.

have a heart attack than the 20 percent of women with the highest levels. And with men, the difference is by a factor of four![8] The conclusion is that the higher your healthy HDL cholesterol levels, the better.
On the other hand, LDL cholesterol correlates with an increased risk of cardiovascular disease, although the relationship is a weak one.
This changes, however, when we break LDL cholesterol down further into the larger particles—also known as "fluffy LDL"—and smaller particles. It turns out that the fluffy particles are harmless and have a neutral effect on the heart and blood vessels; it's the smaller LDL cholesterol particles that are the nasty ones. These smaller particles are not only smaller in size, but their lipoproteins have a high triglyceride content as glucose binds to the protein, and they contain more linoleic acid formed through oxidation. With these changes, the smaller LDL particles become sticky, allowing them to nestle in small tears in the lining of our blood vessels. What follows is chronic inflammation and more tears in the lining. More LDL particles accumulate in the newly formed tears. The lining swells up and eventually closes off the blood vessel leading to an infarction in the tissues beyond the blockage such as the heart and the brain.

We can summarize the characteristics of cholesterol particles with respect to cardiovascular disease as follows:

<u>Total cholesterol level (HDL cholesterol plus LDL cholesterol)</u>
No clear correlation with cardiovascular disease. (However, high total cholesterol levels seem to provide protection from many other conditions)

<u>High HDL cholesterol levels</u>
Decreased risk of cardiovascular disease.

<u>High LDL cholesterol levels (fluffy and small particles together)</u>
Slightly increased risk of cardiovascular disease.

<u>High fluffy LDL cholesterol levels</u>
Neutral.

<u>High small LDL cholesterol levels</u>
Increased risk of cardiovascular disease.

The importance of this subdivision is that, first of all, the HDL, fluffy LDL and smaller LDL particle levels are not influenced by the amount of cholesterol in your diet, but they are influenced by the level of saturated fats and carbohydrates in your nutrition. We've also known for some time that the consumption of saturated fats slightly raises both your LDL and HDL cholesterol levels and hence your total cholesterol. And that's often a sign for your physician to advise you to eat less saturated fat or start using statins. But that advice is unfortunately often misguided! Studies have shown that saturated fats increase, besides the HDL cholesterol levels, only the fluffy LDL levels and not those nasty small LDL particle levels. So in fact, saturated fats increase the quality of the cholesterol you ingest. And that leads us to understand that clinical research has already proven that consuming more saturated fats does not lead to more heart attacks, even though it does increase total cholesterol levels.

Because total cholesterol levels are not a good indicator for evaluating your risk for heart attacks, HDL and LDL cholesterol values nowadays are indicated as separate values in your bloodwork. Physicians often calculate the relationship between the total cholesterol level and the HDL cholesterol levels. Because saturated fats raise the levels of both types of cholesterol, the proportion remains roughly the same when you consume more fats during a ketogenic diet. But proportion doesn't mean everything, because it doesn't take into account the subdivision in LDL cholesterol between the harmless fluffy LDL particles and the harmful smaller particles. Unfortunately, this subdivision of LDL cholesterol into its two variants is not yet a standard lab procedure, so the requesting physician lacks essential information to assess the quality of the cholesterol values in your blood and make an informed decision on whether or not to prescribe statins.

However, there is another indirect method that your physician (and you) can use to get a good impression of the quality of the cholesterol in your blood. And that method also gives you the tools to change your cholesterol values for the better. First of all, know that small LDL particles are produced in the body when you've an increased concentration of triglycerides—a complicated word for fat particles—in your blood.[9]
And your blood triglyceride values are a highly sensitive indicator of your metabolic health. To put it simply: if you constantly eat more carbohydrates than your body can process for its energy needs, your liver will convert the excess carbohydrates into fats. Those are initially stored in the liver. But your liver will gradually accumulate too much fat. It will eventually have to release fats to your bloodstream, where it ends up in the fat tissue in your belly under the skin, where it is stored. This increased transport of fats from the liver to your fatty tissue becomes visible in your blood by the increased triglyceride levels. And how high that level is, is very important, because not only do increased triglyceride levels indicate that your metabolism is off balance, but the more triglycerides you have in your blood, the greater your risk of cardiovascular disease.[10]

And we now have a very good idea of why that's the case, because triglycerides increase the concentration of small LDL cholesterol particles in your blood! Moreover, a raised triglyceride level is almost always the result of sustained high blood sugar levels, which trigger the liver to

9 McNamara J. Jenner J. Li Z. et al. Change in LDL particle size is associated with change in plasma triglyceride concentration. Arterioscler Thromb. 1992; 12(11): 1284-1290.

10 Harchaoui K. Visser M. Kastelein J. et al. Triglycerides and Cardiovascular Risk. *Curr. Cardiol.* Rev. 2009 Aug; 5(3): 216–222.

produce more fat. It's therefore no surprise that the outer lipoproteins of these small LDL particles contain so many triglycerides, making them sticky. And it turns out that lipoproteins in these particles contain a lot of oxidized linoleic acid, which helps produce small, harmful LDL particles at a microscopic level.

The following figure shows how the various types of cholesterol particles are produced (HDL, fluffy LDL and small LDL cholesterol particles).

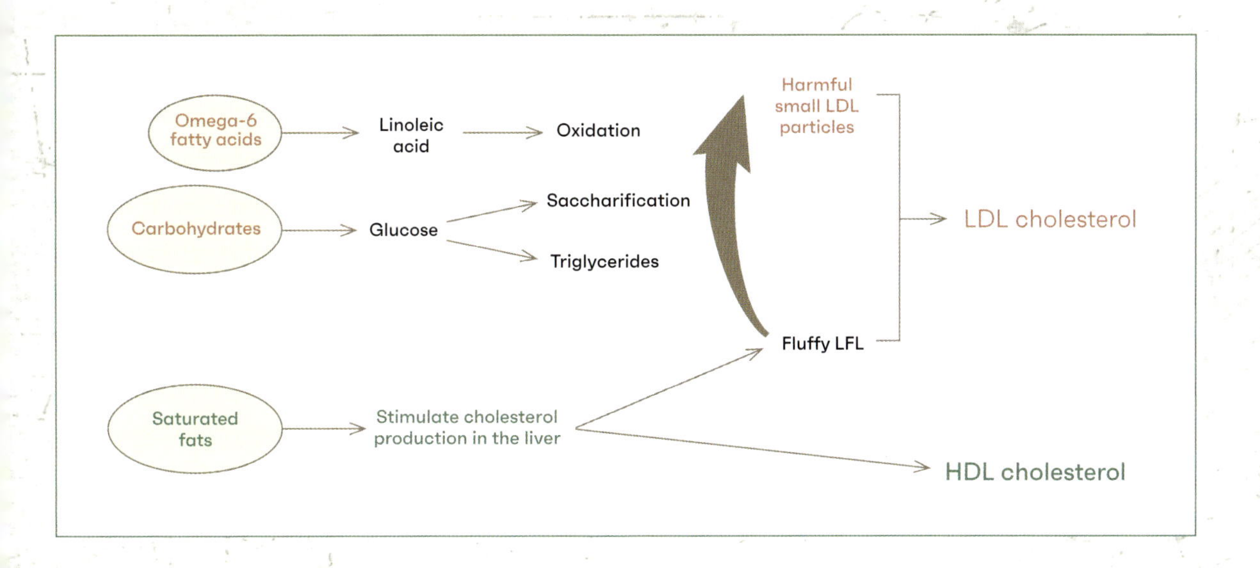

Statins for the treatment of high cholesterol

Physicians generally tend to prescribe statins for high cholesterol levels, particularly when the patient exhibits symptoms of a heart condition. In almost all cases, the statins are to be taken for long periods, often for the rest of a person's life. Sometimes, prescribing statins is the right immediate course of action, but often it's not.

Let's first take a look at why physicians are so eager to prescribe statins. That can best be illustrated with a well-known advertisement from the pharmaceutical company Pfizer about their statin, Lipitor™ (atorvastatin). The advertisement states that when you compare Lipitor to a placebo, the Lipitor group shows a decrease of no less than 36% in the number of fatal heart attacks after four years of treatment. That sounds impressive, and it makes it hard for physicians to justify not prescribing this medication to everyone with even the slightest increased risk of cardiovascular disease. Except, the fine print in the advert gives us some more insight. The information shows that 2 percent of patients in the Lipitor group had died, compared to 3 percent in the placebo group. Although the difference between 2 and 3 explains the relative difference of 36 percent, in absolute numbers this means that the difference of having a deadly heart disease is in effect reduced by 1 percent (3 minus 2 percent) by taking Lipitor. In other words: to prevent 1 fatal heart attack, 100 people require long-term treatment with Lipitor. That sets the statement that Lipitor causes a 36 percent decrease in the number of heart attacks in a whole new light.

So what should you do when your physician tells you that your cholesterol levels are high or too high?

Knowing what you do now, you can ask the right questions. If you want to know how healthy your blood vessels are, you need to know three bloodwork indicators: the total cholesterol level, your HDL cholesterol values and your triglyceride values. And then there are two relationships that count. First of all, divide the total cholesterol level by your HDL cholesterol values, and this value should ideally be around 3.5 or lower. If that value is above 5, you have an increased risk of cardiovascular disease. However, more important than this often-used ratio is the relationship between your triglyceride levels and HDL cholesterol levels. When the value you end up with by dividing your triglyceride value by your HDL cholesterol value is greater than 3, you start to become at risk. You actually want to strive for 2 or lower.

If your physician leans towards prescribing statins, I would advise you to ask your physician to wait a couple of months before prescribing them. During those months, I would first try to adjust my diet: limit the consumption of carbohydrates and avoid linoleic acid as much as possible.
It won't surprise you given the above that I never use liquid cooking oils, which are full of linoleic acid. Replace them with olive oil, butter, ghee, avocado butter and coconut oil. And remove any sugars from your menu! In fact, my general advice is to avoid industrially processed foods altogether and to stay away from the soft drinks and fruit juices. Always choose fresh, unprocessed and full-fat products. It will keep you out of all sorts of trouble. That doesn't mean that you have to switch to a ketogenic diet; you can use any recipe from Pascale's library of cookbooks! You'll see that your triglyceride levels drop radically and your HDL cholesterol levels will rise somewhat. You'll see that the value you end up with when you divide your triglyceride level by your HDL cholesterol level will decrease quickly, and so will your risk of cardiovascular disease. And then you'll discover you don't need statins after all.

I can also recommend exercising more. Exercise is very healthy for your heart and blood in various ways and it usually improves your cholesterol and triglyceride profile, meaning lower triglyceride levels and higher

HDL cholesterol levels. Sometimes lower LDL cholesterol levels are recorded after intensive exercise, but those are less pronounced. All those changes ensure a further decrease in your risk of having a heart attack or stroke. An additional benefit of combining a healthy diet with more exercise is that it may also lower your blood pressure, leading to a reduction in your risk of cardiovascular disease.

A good example of what can happen after a routine bloodwork consultation happened to my own wife, Stacey (56 years). She had a higher cholesterol level than the "normal" upper limit, and her endocrinologist therefore advised her to start taking statins. The relatively high cholesterol values in her blood, however, were primarily caused by a high HDL cholesterol level; her triglyceride levels were very low. That meant that her total cholesterol/HDL cholesterol proportion added up to 2.5 and that of triglycerides/HDL cholesterol a mere 1.3. Those are both excellent values! Moreover, her blood pressure was completely normal (110/70). In other words: Stacey's risk of cardiovascular disease is very low, and so she politely declined the statins.

Conclusion

If you follow a ketogenic diet, your nutrition will mostly consist of fats, including plenty of saturated fats. This will potentially increase your total cholesterol levels. But that's no reason to start worrying, contrary to what many physicians (and dieticians) believe. What happens during a ketogenic diet is that your metabolism improves, leading to a reduction—mostly in triglycerides—and an increase in your healthy HDL cholesterol and neutral fluffy cholesterol levels. And the latter is what you see in your increased LDL cholesterol levels, giving the impression that your "bad" cholesterol levels have increased. That isn't the case, however, because those nasty little LDL particles can't thrive on a ketogenic diet.

So don't let your physician scare you into thinking that your total cholesterol levels are too high or have become too high because of your ketogenic diet when they say your "bad" cholesterol levels have increased. Always ask for more details so you can calculate the proportion of total cholesterol and HDL cholesterol in your blood, and particularly the ratio between triglycerides and HDL cholesterol.

And if you find that those values show unhealthy levels in combination with high LDL cholesterol levels, then it's time to do something about it. And that involves initially changing your diet as described above and exercising more. Only when you discover that these measures don't help, will you know that taking statins is the only option left.

Whatever the case, improving your cholesterol levels by changing your lifestyle is usually far more effective and healthier than having to take medication for the rest of your life.

I took the photographs for this book on the island of Lanzarote. The beautiful light and amazing natural surroundings made it an absolute delight to take pictures.

This is the kitchen where I created all my new recipes for *The Keto Cure 2.* It was such a joy to work in a professional kitchen.

14-DAY MEAL PLANNER

I've created a varied menu, but know that you can switch some of the recipes with alternatives from the "Extra recipes" chapter.

WEEK 1

Day 1
BREAKFAST Delicious omelet with salmon and fresh herbs
LUNCH Sauteed pointed cabbage with juicy cherry tomatoes and melted feta
DINNER Chicken soup with vegetables

Day 2
BREAKFAST Cheese waffles
LUNCH Broccoli soup with halloumi and a Parmesan cheese and walnut crumble
DINNER Fried fish with creamy spinach, tomatoes and olives

Day 3
BREAKFAST Seeds and nuts
LUNCH Sautéed vegetables with egg and bacon
DINNER Hamburger casserole with a lovely thick cauliflower mousse

Day 4
BREAKFAST Chocolate mousse with avocado
LUNCH Tabouleh salad
DINNER Cauliflower risotto with halloumi and Parmesan cheese

Day 5
BREAKFAST Five-minute broccoli omelet
LUNCH Large portobello with spinach, tomatoes and cheese
DINNER Jumbo shrimp with ras-el-hanout and vegetables

Day 6
BREAKFAST Delicious cheese-nut bread with olive oil and herbes de Provence
LUNCH Greek salad with cauliflower rice and feta cheese
DINNER Thai minced beef curry with vegetables

Day 7
BREAKFAST Delicious cheese-nut bread with olive oil and herbes de Provence
LUNCH Delicious salad with squid, avocado and lumpfish roe
DINNER Peanut-coated fried fish with salad

WEEK 2

Day 8	BREAKFAST	Coconut breakfast cake with blueberries
	LUNCH	Avocado with feta and a salad
	DINNER	Fried chicken with mushrooms and Brussels sprouts
Day 9	BREAKFAST	Classic omelet with vegetables
	LUNCH	Mackerel with avocado and greens
	DINNER	Salmon with a lemon-butter sauce and stir-fried vegetables
Day 10	BREAKFAST	Coconut milk with nut paste, strawberries and a nut crumble
	LUNCH	Cauliflower puree with green beans and a poached egg
	DINNER	Shredded pointed cabbage in a creamy cheesy mushroom sauce
Day 11	BREAKFAST	Frittata with spinach and mushrooms
	LUNCH	Spinach with feta and turmeric
	DINNER	Fancy chicken with cauliflower
Day 12	BREAKFAST	Frittata with spinach and mushrooms
	LUNCH	Nori with crayfish and avocado
	DINNER	Endive au gratin with ham in a cauliflower sauce
Day 13	BREAKFAST	Fluffy rolls with ham, cheese ...
	LUNCH	Poke bowl with salmon and cauliflower rice
	DINNER	Asian-style soup with mushrooms and shrimp
Day 14	BREAKFAST	Smoked salmon with avocado, mascarpone and lumpfish roe (with fluffy rolls if you wish)
	LUNCH	Sautéed eggplant with brown shrimp and roasted pine nuts
	DINNER	Sauerkraut with bacon and sausage

You can find the shopping lists on **purepascale.com** or on the Keto Cure Facebook group page.

RECIPES

Week 1

Delicious omelet with salmon and fresh herbs

Preparation time: 10 minutes – Cooking time: 10 minutes

4 eggs
6 tablespoons cream
(1 ¾ oz/50 g)
¾ oz (20 g) sesame seeds
7 oz (200 g) smoked salmon
2 large bunches of fresh herbs
(flat-leaf parsley, dill ...)
2 spring onions

Whisk the eggs together with the cream. Season with salt and pepper and add the sesame seeds. Drizzle a little olive oil in a pan and pour in half the egg mixture. Cover the pan. Keep cooking the omelet until the top is completely dry.
Meanwhile, finely chop the spring onions and combine them with some olive oil and a little salt and pepper. Put half of the salmon slices on top of one half of the omelet and sprinkle half the herbs on top. Fold the omelet over. Garnish the second omelet in the same way.
Sprinkle a few sesame seeds over the top to garnish, if desired.

Per serving: 40.2g P (25.1%) / 3.4g NetC (2.2%) / 51.9g F (72.7%)

An omelet with
a festive touch. :-)

Sauteed pointed cabbage with juicy cherry tomatoes and melted feta

Preparation time: 3 minutes – Cooking time: 12 minutes

1 small pointed cabbage (14 oz/400 g)
15 cherry tomatoes (5 oz/150 g)
5 oz (150 g) feta
1 ¾ oz (50 g) Parmesan cheese
handful of flat-leaf parsley

Slice the pointed cabbage into long strips, starting with the pointed end. Add a generous splash of olive oil to a pan and add the pointed cabbage. Add 4 tablespoons water to the cabbage. Season with salt and pepper. Cover the pan and cook.
Meanwhile, slice the tomatoes in half and add them to the pan. Let everything cook until the cabbage is al dente and the tomatoes have cooked down. Crumble the feta over the vegetables and stir it in.
Finely chop the flat-leaf parsley (keep some aside for the garnish) and stir into the vegetables.
Divide the vegetables over two bowls. Garnish with the Parmesan cheese and some finely chopped flat-leaf parsley.

Tip: Parmesan cheese
Don't have any Parmesan cheese in your kitchen? You can also crumble some extra feta over the top. You're supposed to add 5 ounces/150 grams of feta in so it melts and gives the vegetables a delicious sauce. You can sprinkle some extra cheese on top afterwards; that can be any cheese you like.

With Parmesan cheese, per serving: 28.1g P (22.8%) / 7.7g NetC (6.3%) / 38.8g F (70.9%)
With the feta only, per serving: 21.9g P (19.5%) / 7.6g NetC (6.6%) / 37.1g F (73.9%)

15-minute recipe
This is one of my favorite recipes
because it's ready in no time,
yet it tastes so wonderfully good.

Chicken soup with vegetables

Preparation time: 10 minutes – Cooking time: 20 minutes

2 chicken legs (thigh and drumstick) with skin
2 medium-sized tomatoes (7 oz/200 g)
7 oz (200 g) kale
2 celery stalks (3 ½ oz/100 g)
turmeric

This soup is ready in 30 minutes and is both delicious and healthy.

Pour 3 cups (¾ quart/750 ml) of water into a pan and put the pan over the heat. Place the chicken legs on a work surface and chop them into 3 pieces with a large knife (see tip). Do not remove the fat or skin from the chicken. Put the chicken pieces in the water and make sure that they're fully submerged. Season with salt and pepper and cover the pan.
Slice the celery into small pieces and add them to the pan.
Finely chop and add the kale. Quarter the tomatoes, remove the moisture and seeds from the inside, and add the firm flesh to the soup.
Season with a level tablespoon of turmeric and a couple of grinds of black pepper, if desired.
Cook the soup until the chicken is tender.
Serve immediately.

Tip: cutting chicken thighs
Place the chicken thighs on a chopping board. Take a large, sharp knife. First, slice away the drumstick and then chop the remaining thigh in two. You don't have to hack at the chicken; place your other hand on the knife and press firmly down to cut through the bones.

Tip: kale or spinach
If you can't find kale, replace it with spinach.

Per serving: 37.4g P (28.8%) / 4.9g NetC (3.8%) / 39g F (67.4)%

Cheese waffles

Preparation time: 10 minutes – Cooking time: 10 minutes

For about 5 waffles
2 ½ oz (75 g) grated Cheddar cheese
2 ½ oz (75 g) grated mozzarella
3 ½ oz (100 g) ground almonds
1 egg
1 tablespoon onion powder
¼ tablespoon garlic powder
⅓ oz (10 g) flat-leaf parsley

For the tomato sauce
2 tomatoes

This is a delicious breakfast, but the waffles also make a great appetizer.

Finely chop the flat-leaf parsley.
Put the ground almonds in a bowl. Stir in the egg until you have a thick, dry, dough. Add the cheese, the onion and garlic powder and the parsley, and season with some salt and pepper. Add 1 tablespoon olive oil to the mixture. Knead everything together well. The dough may seem like a dry and lumpy cheesy mass now, but this will sort itself out during the cooking process. Make 4 or 5 balls, put them in the waffle iron and cook until golden brown.
Meanwhile, make the sauce: quarter the tomatoes and remove the moisture and seeds (see tip). Finely chop the flesh, combine with 2 tablespoons olive oil (about 1/3 oz or 10 grams) and season with pepper and salt. Serve the waffles with the tomato sauce.

Tip: cheese
You can also make these waffles with different types of cheese. When you make them with Cheddar and mozzarella, you end up with a lovely cheesy waffle, which I particularly like.

Tip: appetizer
You can also make smaller waffles as a snack or appetizer. In that case, I would serve them without the sauce as a crunchy finger food snack.

If you use this recipe to make 5 cheese waffles, each waffle contains:
15.3g P (21%) / 3.9g NetC (5.5%) / 23.8g F (73.5%)

A heart-warming soup.

Broccoli soup with halloumi and a Parmesan cheese and walnut crumble

Preparation time: 20 minutes – Cooking time: 20 minutes

1 head of broccoli (14 oz/400 g)
¼ celeriac (7 oz/200 g)
7 oz (200 g) halloumi (see tip)

For the crumble
¾ oz (20 g) walnuts
1 oz (30 g) finely grated Parmesan cheese
⅓ oz (10 g) fresh parsley

Cut the florets from the broccoli. Peel and chop the broccoli stem into pieces. Peel the celeriac and chop into pieces.
Put the broccoli and celeriac in a large soup pot and cover with water until everything is just submerged. Add a generous splash of olive oil (3 tablespoons), and season with salt and pepper. Simmer until the vegetables are tender.
Slice the halloumi into pieces and fry them golden brown without fat in a non-stick frying pan. Finely chop the walnuts and parsley and stir them into the Parmesan cheese. Remove a couple of broccoli florets from the soup and then blend the rest to make a thick soup.
Divide the soup over deep dishes and place the broccoli florets and halloumi pieces in the soup. Garnish with the nut crumble and a splash of olive oil.

Tip: celeriac and keto
Although celeriac is a root vegetable—which generally contain more carbs—it doesn't contain that many carbs: between 3.7 and 5 grams of carbs per 100 grams, depending on which carb chart you use. In this recipe, we don't use too much celeriac, just enough to add some lovely texture and a full flavor to this hearty soup.

Tip: keto
This is the keto version of a recipe from one of my other cookbooks, *Echt Eten* (Real Food). We added some more walnuts and Parmesan cheese and a little extra olive oil. And limited the celeriac to 7 ounces (200 grams).

Per serving: 37.7g P (23.6%) / 7.7g NetC (4.8%) / 51g F (71.6%)

Fried fish with creamy spinach, tomatoes and olives

Preparation time: 10 minutes – Cooking time: 20 minutes

2 fish fillets (see tip)
2 oz (60 g) olives (your favorite olives)
5 oz (150 g) cherry tomatoes
10 ½ oz (300 g) spinach
5 fl oz (150 ml) cream (see tip)
2-3 teaspoons (5 grams) ras-el-hanout
dried thyme

Preheat the oven to 350 °F (180 °C).
Finely chop the spinach and put in a baking dish. Cut the cherry tomatoes in half and arrange them on top of the spinach. Add the olives. Season with salt, pepper and dried thyme.
Pour the cream over the top. Bake in the oven for 20 minutes.
Rub the fish fillets in with the ras-el-hanout and cook them in olive oil or butter. Season with salt and pepper.
Arrange the fish on top of the vegetables and serve in the baking dish.

Tip: Which fish should you use?
Haddock, plaice, sole, hake ... All delicious types of fish from our very own North Sea :-).

Tip: cream or coconut milk?
Cream contains almost twice as much fat as coconut milk and about as many carbs. If you tend to get hungry after meals or if you have a very active lifestyle, use cream. If these servings are enough for you, use coconut milk. If you want to lose weight and you're not succeeding, use coconut milk instead of cream. This is how you can play around with the ingredients, depending on your personal needs.

Tip: in a hurry?
If you're strapped for time, place the fish on top of the raw vegetables and cook the fish in the baking dish together with the vegetables. Rub the fish with the spices first, and then with a little olive oil. The ras-el-hanout will give the fish a beautiful color.

Per serving: 36.8g P (26.3%) / 4.7g NetC (3.4%) / 43.7g F (70.3%)

This is one of my favorite recipes; not much work and plenty of flavor.

Seeds and nuts

Preparation time: 10 minutes the first timer, then 2 minutes – Cooking time: none

7 oz (200 g) Greek-style yogurt (or 7 oz/200 g sour cream or coconut milk)
1 tablespoon psyllium fiber (⅓ oz/10 grams) (optional, see tip)

For 2 ¼ oz (60 g) nuts and seeds per person
¾ oz (20 g) pumpkin seeds
¾ oz (20 g) Brazil nuts
¾ oz (20 g) flaxseed
¾ oz (20 g) pecans
¾ oz (20 g) macadamia nuts
¾ oz (20 g) hemp seeds

Coarsely chop the seeds and nuts. Put 3 ½ oz (100 g) full-fat yogurt (or coconut milk or sour cream) in both bowls. Sprinkle 2 ¼ oz (60 g) of the seed-nut mixture over the yogurt and a tablespoonful of psyllium if desired.

Tip: psyllium fiber

Psyllium fiber, or fleawort seeds, is fiber from the fleawort plant. It's used in cooking as a thickening or binding agent in cakes (it's also an ingredient in my fluffy roll recipe on page 142). But the fiber also has health benefits: it acts as a laxative. So if you are having issues with constipation, add a tablespoonful of psyllium. Make sure you drink enough, because the fiber swells up and forms a gelatin-like substance.
There is a lot of confusion about how many carbs psyllium contains. This confusion is due to the fact that fiber is also a form of carbohydrate. But with keto, we only keep track of net carbs; between 0 and 2 grams per 100 grams.

Tip: make more

I always make more of this seed-nut mixture and then store it in a tightly-sealed jar. It's ideal for a quick, easy and delicious breakfast in the mornings! I alternate it with coconut milk, full-fat yogurt or sour cream, depending on what I feel like.
2 ¼ oz (60 g) nuts + Greek-style yogurt
2 ¼ oz (60 g) nuts + coconut milk
2 ¼ oz (60 g) nuts + sour cream

With 3 ½ oz (100 g) full-fat Greek-style yogurt – per serving: 17.2g P (14%) / 6.2g NetC (5.1%) / 44.4g F (81.9%)
With 3 ½ oz (100 g) sour cream – per serving: 13.3g P (8.1%) / 5.2g NetC (3.2%) / 64.4g F (88.7%)
With 3 ½ oz (100 g) coconut milk – per serving: 11.2g P (8.6%) / 4.1g NetC (3%) / 51.6g F (88.4%)

My go-to breakfast:
quick and easy.

Go Nuts

1. Pecans – 4 g C/100 g
2. Brazil nuts – 4 g C/100 g
3. Macadamia nuts – 5 g C/100 g
4. Walnuts – 7 g C/100 g
5. Hazelnuts – 7 g C/100 g
6. Peanuts – 8 g C/100 g
7. Almonds – 9 g C/100 g
8. Pistachios – 15 g C/100 g

Source: dietdoctor.com

Go Seeds

1. Flaxseed – 4 g C/100 g
2. Hemp seeds – 4 g C/100 g
3. Pumpkin seeds – 4 g C/100 g
4. Sunflower seeds – 6 g C/100 g
5. Chia seeds – 9 g C/100 g
6. Pine nuts – 9 g C/100 g
7. Sesame seeds – 10 g C/100 g

Note: if you look up the carb content of seeds, you'll discover that there's a lot of variation depending on which source you use. The above values are an average taken from various carb charts.

EXTRA

Sautéed vegetables with egg and bacon

Preparation time: 15 minutes – Cooking time: 15 minutes

9 oz (250 g) bacon
1/5 head of cauliflower (approx. 7 oz or 200 g)
2 large eggs
3 ½ oz (100 g) zucchini
3 ½ oz (100 g) carrots
handful of flat-leaf parsley

Coarsely chop the cauliflower and sauté in 2 tablespoons olive oil. Season with salt and pepper. Remove the pan from the heat as soon as the cauliflower is tender.
Slice the bacon into pieces and fry them in a different pan in 2 tablespoons olive oil. Dice the carrots and add them to the pan. Stir occasionally. Dice and stir in the zucchini. Once the bacon pieces are cooked, and the vegetables are al dente, add the cauliflower rice. Season with salt and pepper.

Move the vegetables over to one side (or get out another pan and splash a little olive oil in it) and break 1 egg (without beating it first) into the pan. Stir the egg yolk into the egg white as it cooks with a wooden spoon until everything is just cooked through. Move the fried egg over to the side with the vegetables and do the same for the second egg. Season with salt and pepper. Coarsely chop the flat-leaf parsley, toss everything together and serve.

This recipe is inspired by Asian rice stir-fries. Absolutely delicious!

Per serving: 33.9g P (20.6%) / 5.9g NetC (3.6%) / 55.8g F (75.8%)

Hamburger casserole with a lovely thick cauliflower mousse

Preparation time: 25 minutes – Cooking time: 25 minutes

10 ½ oz (300 g) minced beef or pork
1 tablespoon tomato paste (¾ oz/20 g)
3 ½ oz (100 g) pointed cabbage
10 ½ oz (300 g) cauliflower
3 ½ oz (100 g) cream
1 ¾ oz (50 g) mascarpone

Finely chop the pointed cabbage, not in strips but in pieces. Cook the chopped cabbage in a pan with a splash of water and 2 tablespoons olive oil (about ½ oz or 12 grams) (see tip). Season with salt and pepper. Cover the pan. Make sure that the cabbage doesn't dry out and burn. The cabbage should be tender after about 5 minutes. Pour off any leftover moisture. Put the cauliflower in a pan together with a splash of water and 2 tablespoons olive oil (about ½ oz or 12 grams). Season with salt and pepper. Cover the pan and cook until tender. Put the tender cauliflower in a blender or food processor with the cream and mascarpone (season with some extra salt and pepper if desired). Blend until you have a smooth, thick sauce.

Fry the minced beef or pork in butter. Season with salt and pepper. When the minced meat is almost cooked through, add the tomato paste. Briefly fry the tomato paste with the meat before adding the cooked cabbage.

Take a small baking dish. Put the minced meat mixture on the bottom and spoon the cauliflower over the top. Smooth out the cauliflower mousse with the back of a spoon. Briefly put the baking dish under the broiler until the top is a nice golden-brown color. Serve.

Tip: cooking vegetables with olive oil

I always cook my vegetables in a little water with some olive oil. This has nothing to do with adding fat to make the dish keto-proof, and everything to do with flavor. Vegetables that are cooked in a lot of water simply lack flavor and texture. By adding a small amount of water, the vegetables tend to steam and keep their texture. And the extra fat adds flavor because fats enhance natural flavors.

Per serving: 33.7g P (14.5%) / 8.1g NetC (3.4%) / 84.6g F (82.1%)

Delicious casseroles
like this are the ultimate
comfort food: happiness
guaranteed! :-)

THE POWER OF CAULIFLOWER IS ITS VERSATILITY

Cauliflower is back in style again. It has successfully gotten rid of its old-fashioned image. And the latest trends towards low-carb culture have undoubtedly contributed to this revival. Cauliflower is often used as an alternative to carb-rich potatoes or rice.
Cauliflower takes center stage in this book. I've incorporated this vegetable into several recipes because it's such an incredibly versatile ingredient. You can do so much with it that it feels like you're eating something different every time. You can eat cauliflower raw, or you can boil, stir-fry, puree, bake, braise, grill, or serve it as a gratin in a casserole or soup. Moreover, you can combine cauliflower with meat, fish, cheese and much more. A vegetable that can do all that and more deserves appreciation.

What's more, cauliflower is also incredibly healthy, just like most vegetables from the cabbage family. It contains plenty of vitamin C, is an excellent source of minerals, and is rich in phytonutrients such as sulforaphane, a cancer-reducing substance. And cauliflower contains very few carbs: between 2 and 2.7 grams per 100 grams (depending on which carb chart you consult).
This makes cauliflower an ideal keto vegetable.

Chocolate mousse with avocado

Preparation time: less than 10 minutes – Cooking time: none

2 ripe avocados
2 large teaspoons (1 oz/30 g) cocoa powder
7 fl oz (200 ml) coconut milk
10 blueberries
a pinch of ground cinnamon
cocoa nibs (about 5 grams, to garnish)

Put all the ingredients except for the blueberries and cocoa nibs in a blender and blend until smooth.
Divide the mousse over bowls and garnish with the cocoa nibs and the blueberries.

Exceptionally delicious and ready in no time. The raw cocoa nibs give this dish a nice crunchy touch.

Per serving: 9g P (6%) / 4g NetC (1%) / 66g F (93%)

Tabouleh salad

Preparation time: 20 minutes – Cooking time: none

1 ¾ oz (50 g) flat-leaf parsley
2 medium-sized tomatoes
1 ½ oz (40 g) peeled hemp seeds (see tip)
2 spring onions (1 ½ oz/40 g)
1 avocado
1 lime

Quarter the tomatoes and remove the seeds over a sieve to catch the juice (see tip). Dice the fleshy part of the tomato.
Coarsely chop the flat-leaf parsley and finely chop the spring onions. Cut the avocado in half and remove the seed and skin. Cut the flesh into pieces. Put everything into a bowl, add the hemp seeds and lightly toss everything together.
Make the vinaigrette with the tomato juice, 3 tablespoons of olive oil and the juice of half a lime. Season with salt and pepper. Pour over the salad.
Serve the salad with the remaining lime wedges.

Tip: hemp seeds
Hemp seeds come from the well-known hemp plant, but the seeds don't contain enough of the active substances to even get remotely high. You can buy hemp seeds in any health food store. They are nutritious, and peeled hemp seed is soft, which is why I've used it in this recipe as an alternative to bulgur. The down-side to hemp seed is that it's very expensive. You can replace it with almonds if you wish. First chop the almonds into small pieces before soaking them for half an hour to an hour in water; this makes them softer.

Tip: removing the seeds from tomatoes
Place a sieve over a bowl. Quarter the tomatoes, slice away the seeds and let them drop into the sieve. Press the seeds into the sieve so the juice drips into the bowl. We use the juice for the vinaigrette.

Per serving: 10.9g P (10%) / 8.9g NetC (8.1%) / 40.2g F (81.9%)

Raw vegetables make
a delightful change.
Enjoy this delicious
salad with hemp seeds.

Cauliflower risotto with halloumi and Parmesan cheese

Preparation time: 15 minutes – Cooking time: 20 minutes

- 8 oz (225 g) halloumi
- 7 oz (200 g) cauliflower
- 5 oz (150 g) cremini or baby bella mushrooms
- 1 clove of garlic
- 2 tablespoons mascarpone (1 ¾ oz/50 g)
- 1 ¾ oz (50 g) Parmesan cheese
- a few sprigs of thyme
- ¾ oz (20 g) flat-leaf parsley

Finely mince the cauliflower to make cauliflower rice. Grate (or finely chop) the halloumi. Dice the mushrooms into small pieces. Finely chop the garlic and the flat-leaf parsley.
Sauté the mushrooms in butter (¾ oz/20 g) and season with salt and pepper.
Add the garlic. Add the parsley and fresh thyme at the end.
Stir-fry the cauliflower for about 5 minutes until tender in a separate pan with olive oil (see tip). Season with pepper and a little salt (note: Parmesan cheese and halloumi are also salty).
Add the mascarpone, Parmesan cheese and halloumi and stir until everything is mixed in well and you end up with a creamy mixture. Finally stir in the mushrooms.

Divide the risotto over the plates in nice, neat piles and garnish with some fried thyme sprigs.

Tip: frying cauliflower in butter or olive oil?
I prefer to fry the cauliflower in olive oil: butter can turn brown, and I want to keep the cauliflower nice and white.

Tip: fresh thyme
Fresh thyme is such a wonderful herb to cook with. It's also very easy to grow thyme in a pot or in your garden, and it's a winter-hardy plant, just like rosemary. I usually add thyme at the end. Remove some leaves from the sprigs, but you can also add the soft tips of the sprigs; they add an extra decorative touch to the dish.

Per serving: 40.3g P (20.9%) / 7.7g NetC (4%) / 64.4g F (75.1%)

This is a heavenly dish, bursting with flavor.

A quick and tasty breakfast!

Five-minute broccoli omelet

Preparation time: 2 minutes – Cooking time: 3 minutes

For 4 small or
2 large omelets
5 oz (150 g) broccoli florets
4 eggs
1 clove of garlic
any herbs you like: basil, oregano ... (dried or fresh)

Put the broccoli florets, the clove of garlic and the eggs in a blender and blend well.
Season with salt and pepper. Cook the omelets. Garnish with the chopped herbs.

Tip: turning the omelet
As soon as I've poured the eggs into the pan, I cover the pan so the top of the omelet cooks quicker. Wait until the top is dry before turning over the omelet.

Tip: toppings
Serve the omelet with a slice of salmon, cheese, or ham.

Salmon: A little over 1 oz (35 g) per serving
1 omelet with salmon: 23.7g P (27.6%) / 1.3g NetC (1.5%) / 27.1g F (70.9%)

Cheese: A little over 1 oz (35 g) per serving
1 omelet with cheese: 24.6g P (23.7%) / 1.3g NetC (1.2%) / 34.5g F (75.1%)

Cooked ham: A little over 1 oz (35 g) per serving
1 omelet with ham: 23.2g P (29.4%) / 1.5g NetC (1.9%) / 24.1g F (68.7%)

This is a wonderfully
delicious dish and
a feast for the eye.

Large portobello mushroom with spinach, tomatoes and cheese

Preparation time: 5 minutes – Cooking time: 15 minutes

- 2 large portobello mushrooms (7 oz/200 g) (or more smaller ones)
- 7 oz (200 g) spinach
- 7 oz (200 g) cheese (see tip)
- 5 oz (150 g) cherry tomatoes
- ¾ oz (20 g) capers
- ½ oz (15 g) pecans

Take a pan, pour in a little olive oil, and put the portobello mushrooms in with the open side facing up. Pour a little olive oil into the mushroom caps as well. Season with salt and pepper. Cover the pan and cook the mushrooms for about 10 minutes.

Cut the tomatoes in half and cook them in a separate pan in a little olive oil. As soon as they start to release moisture, add the capers and spinach. Cover the pan and let the spinach wilt. Stir the vegetables. Season with salt and pepper. Meanwhile, dice the cheese and add to the vegetable mixture. Let the vegetables heat another minute, covered, until the cheese has just melted. Coarsely chop the pecans.
Divide the vegetables over the portobello mushrooms and garnish with the pecans.

Tip: portobello mushrooms
A portobello mushroom is the adult version of a baby bella or cremini mushroom. If you can't find them, use a smaller variety. In Belgium, we also refer to them as brown mushrooms.

Tip: which cheese should you use?
You can use any cheese you want. I used a semi-mature goat's cheese; this cheese turns soft but doesn't melt all the way through, which I like. You can also use halloumi, which won't melt and keeps its shape. If you want your cheese to completely melt, use a fresh, soft cheese or grated cheese.

Per serving: 29.1g P (16.2%) / 4.4g NetC (2.5%) / 64.5g F (81.3%)

Large shrimp with ras-el-hanout and vegetables

Preparation time: 10 minutes – Cooking time: 10 minutes

14 oz (400 g) organic shrimp with tails (frozen)
2 tomatoes (10 ½ oz/300 g)
10 ½ oz (300 g) spinach
3 ½ fl oz (100 ml) cream
ras-el-hanout

Hold the frozen shrimp under running water and pull them apart. The shrimp can still be frozen, but they should no longer stick together. Heat a pan with a splash of olive oil. Cook the (still frozen) shrimp for about 2 minutes. Sprinkle them with 2 small teaspoons of ras-el-hanout and cook for another two minutes. Meanwhile, slice the tomatoes. Remove the shrimp from the pan, even though they may not be quite cooked through, and transfer them to a plate. Put the tomato slices in the pan with the leftover juices; this gives the tomatoes a delicious flavor. Cover the pan and simmer for 6 to 8 minutes.
Stir the tomatoes and place the spinach on top. Add the cream, cover the pan again and simmer for another 3 minutes. Stir the vegetables and season with salt and pepper to taste.
Place the shrimp on top of the vegetables and cook a little longer to combine all the flavors and the yellow color of the ras-el-hanout. Serve in an attractive serving dish.

A scrumptious dish for when you're strapped for time.

Per serving: 29.7g P (27.6%) / 6g NetC (5.6%) / 32g F (66.8%)

Delicious cheese-nut bread with olive oil and herbes de Provence

Preparation time: 10 to 15 minutes – Cooking time: 40 minutes

Serves 4

7 oz (200 g) ground almonds (see tip)
7 (200 g) grated Emmental cheese
2 tablespoons mascarpone (2 oz/60 g)
2 eggs
1 teaspoon baking soda (see tip on page 215)
herbes de Provence (thyme, rosemary...)

This cheese and nut bread is delicious. Also ideal for lunch on the go. You can eat the bread as it is or top it with some extra cheese or whatever you feel like.

This is also tomorrow's breakfast, which is why we're making a large batch.

Preheat the oven to 350 °F (180 °C).

Combine the ground almonds with the baking soda, season with pepper and a little salt and add the herbes de Provence.

Stir in the mascarpone and the eggs.

Knead the cheese into the nutty flour.

Shape the dough into an oval ¾ inches (1.5 cm) thick. Score the dough crossways and sprinkle plenty of olive oil over the top.

Sprinkle some additional herbes de Provence over the top and bake in the oven for 40 minutes.

Tip: warm or cold

This cheese bread is at its best when served at room temperature. My advice is to bake an extra-large batch. The bread will keep up to 3 days in the refrigerator or longer in the freezer. In both cases, heat the bread briefly in the oven before serving. You'll have a delicious breakfast ready in no time. You can top the bread with cheese or another topping, but it tastes just fine as it is.

Tip: ground almonds

Some people are a bit fed up with the taste of almonds, and if you're not a huge fan of the flavor, that makes perfect sense. But did you know that you can always replace almonds with other kinds of nuts? Hazelnuts are a delicious alternative. Grind them yourself or buy pre-ground hazelnuts in the store.

Per serving: 30.8g P (19%) / 3.3g NetC (2%) / 56.8g F (79%)

This is one of my favorite salads, full of vegetables and rich in flavor. Delicious.

Greek salad with cauliflower rice and feta cheese

Preparation time: 15 minutes – Cooking time: 5 minutes

5 oz (150 g) cauliflower
a handful olives (3 ½ oz/100 g)
1 large tomato (7 oz/200 g)
1 small onion (2 oz/60 g)
6-inch (15 cm) piece of cucumber (about 5 oz/150 g)
handful of flat-leaf parsley
1 packet feta cheese (7 oz/200 g – see tip)
1 lemon

Coarsely chop the cauliflower in a food processor and put the pieces in a pan with 2 tablespoons olive oil, salt and pepper. Stir-fry the cauliflower al dente in a couple of minutes.
Quarter the tomatoes, remove the seeds and catch the juice through a sieve. Dice the flesh into pieces. Cut the cucumber lengthways in two and scrape out the seeds with a spoon. Slice the flesh into half-moons.
Finely chop the parsley and cut the onion into strips.
Put all the vegetables and olives in a bowl, season with salt and pepper and combine well. Crumble the feta over the top.
Combine the tomato juice with the juice of ½ lemon and add 4 tablespoons (1 oz or 24 grams) olive oil. Pour the vinaigrette over the salad. Serve with a wedge of lemon.

Tip: feta

If the portions are generally too large for you or if you're feeling less hungry, use half a packet of feta instead. The opposite also applies; if you're hungry, use more.

Per serving: 19.6g E (11.7%) / 10.2g NetC (6.1%) / 61g F (82.2%)

Thai minced beef curry with vegetables

Preparation time: 15 minutes – Cooking time: 20 minutes

10 ½ oz (300 g) minced beef
1 small onion (2 ¼ oz/70 g)
3 ½ oz (100 g) green beans
7 oz (200 g) pointed cabbage
5 oz (150 g) coconut milk
1 tablespoon red curry paste (1 oz/30 g)
flat-leaf parsley (to garnish)

Slice the beans in half and cook them until tender in a little water with some olive oil (½ oz/15 grams). Cover the pan. Coarsely chop the cabbage and add to the pan. Season with some salt and pepper. Cover again. Check occasionally to make sure the vegetables don't dry out. If they're dry, add a little extra water and/or olive oil.
Season the meat with salt and pepper and form it into 8 meatballs. Fry them in a pan with a little butter (¾ oz/20 grams). Coarsely chop the onion and add to the pan. Once the meat has browned and the onions are soft, add the coconut milk together with the red curry paste. Cook a little longer.
Turn down the heat.
Drain the vegetables and add them to the curry. Serve in deep dishes and garnish with some fresh herbs such as flat-leaf parsley.

Tip: curry paste
Be careful with curry paste: curry pastes can be very spicy depending on which brand you use. The key is to keep tasting. Also, choose a low-carb curry paste. The purer the curry paste, the fewer carbs it contains. :-)

Per serving: 37g P (27.8%) / 9.4g NetC (7.1%) / 38.6g F (65.1%)

This recipe is
always a favorite
for any occasion.

Delicious salad with squid, avocado and lumpfish roe

Preparation time: 15 minutes – Cooking time: none

- 7 oz (200 g) precooked octopus or squid (see tip)
- 2 medium-sized tomatoes (7 oz/200 g)
- 1 ripe avocado
- 1 small onion (1 ½ oz/50 g)
- ⅓ oz (10 g) chives
- ¾ oz (20 g) lumpfish eggs
- 1 lime
- 2 to 3 tablespoons light soy sauce

Cut the octopus or squid into pieces. Quarter the tomatoes, remove the seeds and catch the juice through a sieve. Dice the flesh into pieces. Cut the avocado in half, remove the seed, and spoon out the inside. Dice the avocado. Cut the onion in half and slice into long strips. Finely chop the chives.
Combine everything in a bowl and season with sea salt and black pepper.
Add the juice of ½ lime, 2 to 3 tablespoons soy sauce and 3 tablespoons olive oil.
Halve the remaining wedge of lime and serve it next to the salad.

Tip: squid
Squid tentacles, pulpo, or octopus, all refer to the same type of ingredient. I love its taste and texture; squid is delicious. You can find it in the supermarket and at the fish market. You can also replace it with precooked calamari or prawns.

This is a delightfully fresh salad that everyone loves.

Per serving: 20.9g P (19.9%) / 9.2g NetC (8.8%) / 33.4g F (71.3%)

Peanut-coated fried fish with salad

Preparation time: 15 minutes – Cooking time: 15 minutes

2 small firm fish fillets (see tip)
1 oz (30 g) peanuts
1 egg

For the salad (see tip)
12 small tomatoes (4 oz/120 g)
2 spring onions
large handful of coriander (¾ oz/20 g) (see tip)
1 lime
2 tablespoons soy sauce

Finely chop the coriander.
Beat the egg lightly in a deep dish and stir the finely chopped coriander into the egg. Coarsely grind the peanuts and put them on a flat plate.
Heat a pan with a large knob of butter or coconut oil (¾ ounces/ 20 grams). Make sure the fat is nice and hot (but not burning: the fat shouldn't be so hot that it smokes). First coat the fish fillets with the egg, followed by the peanuts, and then place them in the pan. Season with salt and pepper. Turn them over only once.

For the salad, chop the tomatoes in half, finely chop the spring onions, and toss to combine. Add the coriander. Pour 2/3 table-spoon (½ ounce/15 grams) olive oil, the juice of ½ lime and 2 tablespoons soy sauce into the mixture. Combine well.
Serve the fish and the salad with a wedge of lime.

Tip: which fish should you use?
Choose a firm fish fillet, such as sea bass, sole or salmon... get a small fillet, because the egg and peanuts make this a filling meal.

Tip: coriander
If you think coriander tastes like soap :-), replace it with flat-leaf parsley.

Tip: salad
Feel free to add any keto-friendly raw vegetables to this salad, such as cucumber, green lettuce, endive, green asparagus, avocado ...

Per serving: 40.4g P (32.5%) / 5.5g NetC (4.4%) / 34.9g F (63.1%)

The peanuts and
coriander give this
dish an Asian touch.

RECIPES

Week 2

Coconut breakfast cake with blueberries

Preparation time: 10 minutes
Cooking time: 30 minutes

1 oz (30 g) coconut flour
3 ½ oz (100 g) coconut milk
1 oz (30 g) melted coconut oil
2 eggs
2 ¾ oz (80 g) blueberries
a couple of drops of vanilla extract to taste (optional)
lemon zest (see tip)

Extra: baking parchment + 6-inch (16 cm) round cake pan

Preheat the oven to 350 °F (180 °C).
Combine the coconut flour, coconut oil and coconut milk. Whisk in the eggs. Grate some lemon zest over the dough (see tip), add vanilla extract if desired, and combine. Finally, stir in the blueberries.

Line a small baking pan with baking parchment Mine has a diameter of about 6 inches (16 cm).
Put the dough inside the pan, making sure that some of the berries are sitting on top. Bake in the oven for about 30 minutes. Don't bake the cake too long or it will dry out.

Tip: lemon zest
Wash the lemon thoroughly and only use the yellow part of the peel (the white part tastes bitter). This gives the cake a hint of freshness without making it too sour. If you don't have any lemons lying around, don't worry. You can simply leave it out.

Tip: no time in the mornings?
Make some more to last you several days. The cake will keep up to 3 or 4 days in the refrigerator. You can also freeze the cake.
Let the cake defrost and heat it up in the oven under aluminum foil, if desired. This should take about 10 to 15 minutes.

Tip: no sugar
Coconut flour and coconut milk already have that slightly sweet flavor, and the berries add sweetness as well. You really don't have to add any sweeteners to this cake. And I don't think it's a good habit to sweeten your breakfast every time. After all, we're trying to get rid of that craving for something sweet. Learn to appreciate natural flavors.

Per serving: 11.3g P (12.3%) / 8.1g NetC (8.7%) / 32.1g F (79%)

A delicious breakfast
and a welcome change,
especially if you
love coconut.

Avocado with feta and a salad

Preparation time: 15 minutes – Cooking time: none

1 ripe avocado
1 packet of feta (7 oz/200 g)
handful chives
juice of ½ lemon
2 tomatoes
lettuce

Spoon the flesh from the avocado and put it in a bowl. Crumble the feta over the top. Finely chop the chives (set some aside for the garnish) and add to the avocado mixture. Season with black pepper and a little salt and add the lemon juice. Combine well.

Slice the tomatoes into wedges. Divide the lettuce over the plates and arrange the tomatoes on top. Season with salt and pepper and drizzle some olive oil over the top. Spoon the avocado-feta mixture into the middle.
Garnish with the leftover chopped chives.

Avocado puree is delicious, but I find it's always missing something. Add feta or mascarpone and you suddenly have this gorgeous rich flavor.

Per serving: 19.1g P (14%) / 9.4g NetC (7%) / 47.8g F (79%)

One of those perfect
dishes for when you're
short on time.

A very natural
combination of flavors that
complement each other.

Pan-fried chicken with mushrooms and Brussels sprouts

Preparation time: 15 minutes – Cooking time: 20 minutes

- 2 chicken breasts
- 7 oz (200 g) cremini or baby bella mushrooms
- 2 cloves of garlic
- 7 oz (200 g) Brussels sprouts
- juice of ½ lemon or lime
- ras-el-hanout
- flat-leaf parsley (to garnish)

Cut the chicken breasts into pieces and brown them in butter (1 oz/30 grams). Meanwhile, slice the mushrooms and add them to the pan. Season with salt and pepper. Pour some olive oil (½ oz/15 grams) over the mushrooms. Cover the pan for about 5 minutes; the pan will steam up, which speeds up the cooking process, while the moisture prevents the chicken from burning. Meanwhile, finely chop the garlic and add it into the pan. Continue to cook uncovered. Stir regularly. Add extra olive oil if needed.

Remove the outer leaves from the Brussels sprouts and quarter them. Put them in a pan with a little water and 2 tablespoons olive oil (¾ oz/20 g), a small teaspoonful ras-el-hanout and some salt and pepper. Stir well so the Brussels sprouts turn a nice even color.
Cover the pan and cook for 3 to 5 minutes. Add the lemon juice and keep cooking, uncovered, until all the moisture has evaporated.

Add the Brussels sprouts to the chicken. Garnish with some finely chopped flat-leaf parsley. Serve.
Bon appetit!

Per serving: 40.4g P (32.5%) / 5.5g NetC (4.4%) / 34.9g F (63.1%)

Classic omelet with vegetables

Preparation time: 15 minutes – Cooking time: 15 minutes

6 cremini or baby bella mushrooms
14 cherry tomatoes
4 large eggs
1 ¾ oz (50 g) butter
flat-leaf parsley (optional, to garnish)

Put a knob of butter (¾ oz/20 g) in a pan and put the whole mushrooms in together with the tomatoes. Cook the vegetables slowly, covered, over low heat. Season with salt and pepper.

Beat 2 eggs. Place a knob of butter (½ oz/15 g) into a separate pan, let the butter melt and pour in the eggs. As soon as the bottom layer starts to set, roll the omelet with a spatula from the one side to the other, like rolling up a curtain. The egg shouldn't be completely dry on top. The art is to take the omelet off the heat at exactly the right moment. Season with salt and pepper. Garnish with some flat-leafed parsley, if desired.
Do the same for the second omelet.
Serve with the cooked vegetables and some keto bread if you wish.

Tip: keto bread on the side?
If you are trying to lose weight and you're not succeeding, don't add bread to this dish, or keep it minimal.

Nothing beats a classic omelet. The trick is to remove the omelet from the heat just in time before it becomes too dry.

Per serving: 21.3g P (19.8%) / 3g NetC (2.8%) / 36.9g F (77.4%)
Per serving with a fluffy roll (page 142): 30g P (19.2%) / 4.7g NetC (3%) / 54g F (77.8%)

The edible flower is a pansy; I found it in my mixed lettuce.

Mackerel with avocado and greens

Preparation time: 6 minutes – Cooking time: none

10 ½ oz (300 g) smoked mackerel
1 avocado
mixed lettuce

An ideal keto lunch for when you don't have much time.

Toss the lettuce and olive oil together and season with salt and pepper.
Divide the avocado flesh and the mackerel over the plates.

Tip: mackerel
When you follow a keto diet, you need to plan ahead. You should never be in a position where you don't have anything in your kitchen that fits into your keto diet, so you can always make a delicious keto meal. Mackerel is one of those perfect ingredients for keeping around. I always have a smoked mackerel in my pantry (also for my moderately low-carb dishes). It's exceptionally delicious and healthy, and it keeps for quite a while.

Tip: recipe
This is a last-minute recipe. It takes practically no time to make, is ideal for on the go and is just a fabulous all-round keto recipe; it contains very few carbs and plenty of healthy fats.

Per serving: 33g P (22%) / 53g V (77%) / 2g NetC (1%)

Salmon with a lemon-butter sauce and stir-fried vegetables

Preparation time: 20 minutes – Cooking time: 15 minutes

2 salmon fillets
1 oz (30 g) butter
1 lemon
handful of curly-leaf parsley

7 oz (200 g) spinach
7 oz (200 g) mushrooms
10 cherry tomatoes
(4 ½ oz/140 g)
2 tablespoons capers
1 clove of garlic

Roll up the spinach leaves and finely shred them. Slice the mushrooms. Slice the cherry tomatoes in half. Finely chop the garlic and the curly-leaf parsley.

Put the butter in the pan and fry the salmon fillets over medium heat. Add the lemon juice after a couple of minutes. Season with salt and black pepper and let it simmer slowly a bit longer. Turn the fish over once or twice. Add some of the finely chopped parsley at the end.

Add a generous splash of olive oil to another pan and fry the mushrooms first. After about 2 minutes, add the tomatoes, garlic, and capers. As soon as the tomatoes start to soften, add the spinach. Season with salt and pepper.

Divide the vegetables over the plates and place the salmon next to the vegetables. Spoon the lemon-butter sauce over the fish.

Tip: how long should you cook salmon?
My favorite way to cook salmon is until the inside is no longer raw but is still slightly translucent. It is important to cook the salmon over medium heat, so the lemon juice caramelizes without burning.

Per serving: 32.7g E (20.5%) / 4.7g NetC (3%) / 54.2g F (76.5%)

This delicious
lemon-butter sauce
almost tastes sweet.

Coconut milk with nut paste, strawberries, and a nut crumble

Preparation time: 10 minutes – Cooking time: none

10 ½ fl oz (300 ml) coconut milk (see tip)
4 teaspoons nut paste (1 ¾ oz/50 g) (see tip)
2 oz (60 g) strawberries
¾ oz (20 g) mixed nuts (hazelnuts, Brazil nuts, pecans, walnuts ...)

Take 2 glasses. First, pour in some coconut milk and spoon a teaspoonful of nut paste into the milk. Pour in some more coconut milk, add another teaspoonful of nut paste and finish with the milk.
Briefly stir the nut paste and coconut milk together.
Coarsely chop the strawberries and divide them over the glasses.
Garnish with some coarsely chopped nuts.

Tip: coconut milk or something else?
The thicker the coconut milk, the thicker the result. You can also alternate it with full-fat yogurt, sour cream, mascarpone or ricotta.

Tip: nut paste
You have nut paste with plenty of carbs and with fewer carbs. Nut paste made from almonds usually contains the fewest carbs, about 6 grams per 100 grams.

With 10 ½ oz (300 g) coconut milk – per serving: 11g P (8.4%) / 6.9g NetC (5.3%) / 50.3g F (86.3%)
With 10 ½ oz (300 g) full-fat yogurt – per serving: 15.4g P (14.9%) / 8.6g NetC (8.2%) / 35.4g F (76.9%)
With 10 ½ oz (300 g) mascarpone – per serving: 15.8g P (7.4%) / 9.7g NetC (4.6%) / 83.7g F (88%)
With 10 ½ oz (300 g) sour cream – per serving: 11.8g P (7.1%) / 7.3g NetC (4.4%) / 65.4g F (88.5%)
With 10 ½ oz (300 g) ricotta – per serving: 25.8g P (21.7%) / 7.7g NetC (6.6%) / 37.8g F (71.7%)

A quick and
delicious breakfast.

Cauliflower puree with green beans and a poached egg

Preparation time: 20 minutes – Cooking time: 15 minutes

- 9 oz (250 g) cauliflower
- 5 oz (150 g) green beans
- 2 or 4 market-fresh eggs (depending on how hungry you are)
- ¾ oz (20 g) flat-leaf parsley
- 1 ¾ oz (50 g) mascarpone

Cook the cauliflower in a splash of water and 2 tablespoons olive oil (about ½ ounce or 12 grams). Season with salt and pepper. Cover the pan. Put the tender cauliflower in a blender or food processor and blend with the mascarpone to make a smooth puree. Season with some salt and pepper if desired.

Cook the green beans separately in a little water with some olive oil in a covered pan. (Note: the beans need longer to cook, so you can add a bit more water here). Once the beans are tender, drain off the remaining water if necessary. Return the pan to the heat, add 2 tablespoons olive oil (½ ounce/12 grams) and fry them a little longer. Season with salt and pepper. Coarsely chop some flat-leaf parsley and add to the pan.

Gently bring a pan of water to a boil. Break an egg in a large wooden spoon and slowly dip the spoon into the water (this is by far the easiest way to poach an egg). Do the same for the other eggs. Let the eggs simmer for about 3 minutes.

Spoon the cauliflower puree onto a plate and make a well in the middle with the back of a spoon. Place the egg in the well and arrange the beans on the side.

Serving a poached egg has never been this easy or fun. And it goes wonderfully with the creamy cauliflower.

Per serving with 1 egg: 12.7g P (12.7%) / 6.7g NetC (6.7%) / 36.1g F (80.6%)
Per serving with 2 eggs: 19.2g P (16.1%) / 6.7g NetC (5.6%) / 41.5g F (78.3%)

Shredded pointed cabbage in a creamy cheesy mushroom sauce

Preparation time: 15 minutes – Cooking time: 15 minutes

- 10 ½ oz (300 g) pointed cabbage
- 10 ½ oz (300 g) cremini or baby bella mushrooms
- handful of flat-leaf parsley
- 5 oz (150 g) cream
- 2 ¾ oz (80 g) grated Emmental cheese
- ¾ oz (20 g) Parmesan cheese

Slice the pointed cabbage into long strips, starting from the top of the cabbage and shred . Cook the shredded cabbage in a covered pan with a splash of water and 2 tablespoons olive oil. Stir occasionally. Season with salt and pepper.

Slice the mushrooms and fry them in 3 tablespoons olive oil. Season with salt and pepper.

Coarsely chop the parsley and add to the mushrooms (be careful: this may spatter).

In a separate pan, heat the cream and melt the grated Emmental cheese in the cream. Stir well until you have a smooth and creamy sauce. Pour away any leftover moisture from the cabbage and add the cheese sauce. Stir in the mushrooms. Serve with grated Parmesan cheese.

This is a delicious and fun recipe for those days when you don't feel like fish or meat.

Per serving: 25.1g P (13.3%) / 6.2g NetC (3.3%) / 69.9g F (83.4%)

Frittata with spinach and mushrooms

Preparation time: 15 minutes – Cooking time: 30 minutes

Serves 4
10 ½ oz (300 g) mushrooms
1 lb (450 g) fresh spinach
3 cloves of garlic
9 eggs
7 oz (200 g) sour cream
4 oz (120 g) finely grated Parmesan cheese

Extra: baking parchment

Preheat the oven to 350 °F (180 °C).
Slice the mushrooms and sauté them in plenty of olive oil in a wok. Add the spinach as soon as the mushrooms are cooked.
Finely chop the fresh garlic. Beat the eggs, sour cream, grated Parmesan cheese and garlic together.
Line a baking dish with baking parchment. Put the vegetables in the baking dish, smooth the top down and pour the egg mixture over the top. Bake in the oven for 30 minutes.
Serve warm or cold.

Tip: Ideal to take with you.
This dish is also perfect for taking with you when you're on the go. You can also make your own variation with other low-carb vegetables. You can also freeze the frittata in individually sized servings, so you always have something at home for those unexpected moments.

Per serving: 31.8g P (22.6%) / 3.3g NetC (2.3%) / 46.9g F (75.1%)

A frittata always tastes good. We make an extra big batch for tomorrow morning as well.

Spinach with feta and turmeric

Preparation time: 10 minutes – Cooking time: 10 minutes

14 oz (400 g) fresh spinach
1 packet of feta (7 oz/200 g)
2 cloves of garlic
1 teaspoon turmeric
10 ½ oz (300 g) cremini or baby bella mushrooms

Clean the mushrooms and slice them into large pieces.
Finely chop the garlic and crumble the feta.
Pour plenty of olive oil (3 tablespoons) in a pan, add the turmeric and set the pan over medium heat. Season generously with black pepper (make sure that the turmeric doesn't burn). Add the garlic, and once it turns translucent, the spinach. Once the spinach has completely wilted, sprinkle the feta over the top. Stir well.
The feta will partially melt.
Delicious!
Meanwhile, cook the mushrooms in a separate pan in plenty of olive oil. Season with salt and pepper. Place the spinach in the middle of a plate and arrange the mushrooms around the spinach.

Note: mushrooms
Most mushrooms are keto friendly, except for shiitake mushrooms. Choose cremini or baby bella mushrooms, the light-brown variety of the classic white mushroom, and you're always on track. This mushroom contains about 0.6 g NetC/100 g.

This is, without a doubt, one of my favorite dishes. It's quick to make, looks fabulous and is rich in flavor.

Per serving: 22.6g P (17.5%) / 3.7g NetC (2.9%) / 45.3g F (79.6%)

This dish always looks wonderful when served on a large platter.

Fancy chicken with cauliflower

Preparation time: 15 minutes – Cooking time: 20 minutes

10 ½ oz (300 g) chicken breasts
⅓ head of cauliflower (approx. 10 ½ oz or 300 g)
1 tablespoon tomato paste (¾ oz/20 g)
3 ½ fl oz (100 ml) cream
1 tablespoon red curry paste (¾ oz/20 g)
handful of flat-leaf parsley (garnish)

Not too much work and plenty of flavor. :-)

Slice the cauliflower into florets and put the pieces in a pan with 2 tablespoons olive oil, salt and pepper. Cover the pan and cook until tender (see tip).
Slice the chicken into pieces and fry them in olive oil or coconut oil. Season with salt and pepper.
Combine the tomato paste with the red curry paste and cream. When the chicken is tender, add the tomato sauce. Finally, gently stir in the tender cauliflower florets.
Garnish with some flat-leaf parsley.

Tip: chicken
I actually prefer to use chicken thighs. They have much more flavor because they have more fat. The downside is that it takes some work removing the bone from the thigh. You can also ask your butcher to do it for you.

Tip: cooking vegetables
How I cook vegetables: I put the vegetables in a pan and add water until they are about ⅕ submerged. I season the vegetables with salt and pepper and add a splash of olive oil. I cover the pan when I cook them so the vegetables are partly steamed. The water has usually evaporated by the end of cooking time. If not, then I drain off any remaining water. I like to cook my vegetables al dente and not overcook them. :-)

Per serving: 39.9g P (29.5%) / 7.7g NetC (5.7%) / 39.1g F (64.8%)

DAY 12 – BREAKFAST – Frittata with spinach and mushrooms, page 132.

DAY 12 – LUNCH From: *Low Carb Cookbook 1*

Nori with crawfish and avocado

Preparation time: 15 minutes – Cooking time: none

10 ½ oz (300 g) precooked crawfish
1 avocado
2 sheets nori seaweed
4 spring onions
coarse salt

Preheat the oven to 350 °F (180 °C).
Coat the nori sheets on one side with olive oil and scatter some coarse salt over the top. Roast the sheets in the oven for about 3 minutes (see tip). Cut the avocado in half, remove the seed and spoon out the inside. Put the avocado in a bowl and roughly chop into small pieces with a knife. Add the crawfish. Finely chop the spring onions and add them to the mixture.
Toss everything together and season with salt and pepper.
Place the nori sheet shiny side down on your worktop. Place the avocado mixture at the bottom of the sheet and roll up firmly. Slice the roll into two pieces and serve.

Tip: roasting nori

You can skip this step, but roasted nori is crispier and tastier. If you don't roast the nori, it will soak up the moisture more quickly, making the nori tough and harder to bite into.

Tip: on the go?

If you're making this beforehand for lunch on the go, I would recommend adding a little lemon juice so the avocado keeps its fresh, green color. 1 tablespoon lemon juice contains about 0.7 grams carbs.

Per serving (half the recipe): 31.8g P (23.5%) / 7.8g NetC (5.7%) / 42.6g F (70.8%)

Ideal to take with you, and ready in 15 minutes!

4 heads of endive
(a little over 1 lb/500 g)
4 slices of cooked ham
(7 oz/200 g)
3 ½ fl oz (100 ml) cream
7 oz (200 g) cauliflower
1 ¾ oz (50 g) Emmental cheese
nutmeg

A classic dish, but deliciously different.

Preheat the oven to 350 °F (180 °C).
Cut the endive heads in half and sauté them in butter (¾ ounce/20 grams) with a generous splash of water. Cover the pan to speed up the cooking process. Turn them over only once. Season with salt, pepper and nutmeg.
Meanwhile, cook the cauliflower in a splash of water and 2 tablespoons olive oil.
The endive should be cooked through after 25 to 30 minutes. Remove the cooked endive from the pan, place two halves on a slice of cooked ham, roll them up and place them in a baking dish. Drain the cauliflower and blend it together with the cream to create a smooth sauce. Season with salt and pepper. Spoon the sauce over the endive rolls. Sprinkle the Emmental cheese over the top and broil the dish for about 10 minutes in the oven until the top is nice and bubbly.
Serve immediately in the baking dish.

Tip: what's the story on combining different protein sources?
For example: cheese together with meat, or fish with meat. You may have noticed that you won't often find combinations like this in my earlier books. Not so much for health reasons (science has nothing bad to say about this combination, but nothing positive either), but because it's more a personal choice. I love pure flavors. Combining proteins makes a dish unnecessarily rich. And you end up eating lots of protein, sometimes too much, and that's not good.
So, I'm not against combining proteins as such—and some combinations are just delicious, like in this recipe—but then I try to adjust the amounts accordingly and use less meat.

Per serving: 35.9g P (23.6%) / 9.2g NetC (6.1%) / 47.7g F (70.3%)

Endive au gratin with ham in a cauliflower sauce

Preparation time: 10 minutes – Cooking time: 40 minutes

Fluffy rolls

Preparation time: 10 minutes – Cooking time: 40 minutes

For about 7 rolls

- 7 oz (200 g) ground almonds (see tip)
- 2 oz (60 g) psyllium fiber
- 1 level teaspoon baking soda (see tip on page 215)
- 2 egg whites
- sesame seeds (garnish)

These are perfect "passe-partout" rolls; you can combine them with almost anything, fluffy on the inside and slightly crispy on the outside. You can top them with tapenade, cheese or cold cuts.

Preheat the oven to 350 °F (180 °C).

Combine the ground almonds with the psyllium fiber. Add the baking soda, a little salt and pepper and a tablespoonful of olive oil. Stir briefly. Heat a little over 1 cup (250-300 ml) water until it's lukewarm and then knead it into the mixture. Add the egg whites and knead them into the dough. The dough may feel slippery and clumpy at first, but keep kneading until you end up with a ball shape. Shape the dough into 7 or 8 smaller balls. Place the balls on parchment paper on a baking sheet and sprinkle some sesame seeds as garnish over the top. Bake in the oven for about 40 minutes. Serve the rolls with butter and ham, or salmon ...

Tip: storage

The rolls will keep up to 3 days in the refrigerator. Pop them briefly in the oven to make them light and crispy again. You can also freeze them. Allow the rolls to defrost first before heating them in the oven.

Tip: ground almonds

You can also use another type of ground nuts. I often make them with ground hazelnuts as well. Grind the nuts yourself or buy pre-ground nuts at the store.

Tip: egg whites

The egg whites are essential because they contain amino acids that make sure the baking soda does its work and makes the rolls light and fluffy. (See tip on page 215)

Tip: fake bread

Was bread and cake your nemesis when you were eating the way you used to (as was the case with me)? Then I recommend limiting bread and cake in your keto diet, even though it won't kick you out of ketosis. Because otherwise you won't learn to change your eating habits. Your craving for bread and cake will remain and you'll never succeed in achieving what you want: losing weight and learning to eat differently.

If you make 7 rolls from this recipe, then each serving contains:
8.7g P (17.8%) / 1.6g NetC (3%) / 17.3g F (79.2%)
Roll with ¾ oz/20 g cheese: 13.8g P (20.1%) / 1.6g NetC (2.2%) / 23.6g F (77.7%)
Roll with ¾ oz/20 g ham: 13g P (24%) / 1.8g NetC (3.2%) / 17.6g F (72.8%)
Roll with ¾ oz/20 g salmon: 13.3g P (22.7%) / 1.6g NetC (2.6%) / 19.3g F (74.7%)

Poke bowl with salmon and cauliflower rice

Preparation time: 20 minutes – Cooking time: 4 minutes

¼ head of cauliflower (about 7 oz or 200 g)
7 oz (200 g) salmon fillet without skin
1 avocado
6-inch (15-cm) piece of cucumber
1 lime
4 tablespoons soy sauce
2 spring onions
4 radishes
lettuce
sesame seeds to garnish (⅓ oz/10 g)

The poke bowl originally comes from Hawaii. Today, it's become a trendy word for raw, fresh fish with various vegetables.

Finely chop the cauliflower in a food processor. Put the cauliflower rice in a pan together with 2-3 tablespoons olive oil and sauté until al dente. Season with salt and pepper. Set the rice aside and allow it to cool.
Dice the salmon into cubes and marinate them in 2 tablespoons soy sauce, 2 tablespoons olive oil and the juice of half a lime. Season with pepper only.
Cut the avocado in half, remove the seed, and slice the flesh into wedges.
Slice the radishes into thin slices and the spring onions into rings.
Slice the cucumber in half lengthways and remove the seeds with a teaspoon. Slice the flesh into half-moons. Tap on the cucumber pieces with a wooden spoon or another solid object to bruise them slightly. Put the cucumber pieces in a bowl and pour 2 tablespoons soy sauce and 2 tablespoons olive oil over the top. Season with black pepper and sprinkle some sesame seeds over the top.

Arrange a few lettuce leaves on the plates. Divide the cauliflower and the rest of the vegetables over the top and then place the fish in the middle. Serve with a wedge of lime on each plate.

Tip: vegetables
You can add any keto-friendly vegetables to this dish: cucumber, diced tomato, cooked green beans, seaweed ...

Tip: poke bowl
"Poke-ay!" That's what you'll hear fishermen on Hawaii shout to refer to the freshly cut chunks of the catch of the day. These chunks are usually served with vegetables and sticky rice. We've replaced the sticky rice with cauliflower rice. Today, the poke bowl has conquered the world and there are countless variations out there. The fresh raw fish, on the other hand, is always a staple ingredient.

Per serving: 26.5g P (16.4%) / 9.7g NetC (6%) / 55.8g F (77.6%)

Asian-style soup with mushrooms and shrimp

Preparation time: 10 minutes – Cooking time: 12 minutes

10 ½ oz (300 g) mushrooms (see tip)
14 oz (400 g) jumbo shrimp or scampi
10 ½ fl oz (300 ml) runny coconut milk

For the herbs
2 lemongrass stalks
½-inch (1 cm) piece of ginger root
1 clove of garlic
¼ red chili pepper (optional)
handful of fresh coriander

Slice the large mushrooms in pieces; leave the smaller ones whole. Sauté them for about 3 minutes in plenty of olive oil. Meanwhile, finely chop the ginger, garlic and chili pepper and add them to the mushrooms. Season with salt and plenty of pepper.
Bruise the lemongrass stalks; place the blade of the knife on the stalks and press down with the palm of your hand. Add the lemongrass to the mushrooms and pour in the coconut milk and an equal amount of water (see tip).
Let the soup simmer gently for a couple of minutes. Don't add the shrimp until the end. They only need to cook for a few minutes, just until they're opaque.
Stir in the coarsely chopped coriander just before serving.

Tip: how much coconut milk?
That's hard to determine because some types of coconut milk can be very creamy while others can be very runny. I buy runny coconut milk for this dish and add equal amounts of coconut milk and water. The best way to check is to taste the soup.
Let everything simmer gently and then taste the soup. If the soup tastes watery, add more coconut milk.

Tip: which mushrooms should you use?
Most mushrooms are keto-friendly and contain between 0.5 and 3.5 grams carbs per 100 grams. I'd be careful with shiitake mushrooms, though; they contain about 4.5 grams carbs per 100 grams, and some charts report higher levels. Dried versions can even contain up to 24 grams per 100 grams. You can't go wrong with cremini or baby bella mushrooms, with just 0.6 grams per 100 grams.

Per serving: 28.7g P (22.2%) / 4.7g NetC (3.7%) / 42.7g F (74.1%)

I love Asian flavors, colors and scents. When I long for those typical Asian flavors, lemongrass does wonders. Bruise the stalk and let it simmer with the dish; it gives your dishes a deep, fresh flavor and it's a touch subtler than lime.

Smoked salmon, avocado, mascarpone and lumpfish roe

Preparation time: 10 minutes – Cooking time: none

7 oz (200 g) smoked salmon
1 ripe avocado
2 tablespoons mascarpone (2 oz/60 g)
1 spring onion
2 teaspoons lumpfish roe (¾ oz/20 g)

Put the avocado flesh together with the mascarpone in a blender and mix to an even puree. Season with salt and pepper.
Thinly slice the spring onions.
Arrange the salmon on the plates, divide the avocado-mascarpone mixture over the salmon and sprinkle some of the spring onion on top. Garnish with the lumpfish roe.

The combination of avocado and mascarpone is so surprisingly delicious, it's almost magical. A perfect morning treat!

Per serving: 26.8g P (22.3%) / 4.1g NetC (3.3%) / 39.5g F (74.4%)

Sautéed eggplant with brown shrimp and roasted pine nuts

Preparation time: 15 minutes – Cooking time: 15 minutes

1 large eggplant
7 oz (200 g) precooked brown shrimp
1 oz (30 g) pine nuts
¾ oz (20 g) curly-leaf parsley

Don't hesitate to make this, because it's absolutely amazing!

Slice the eggplant lengthwise into four slices. Fry the eggplant in a non-stick pan in 5 tablespoons olive oil and season with salt and pepper. After a couple of minutes, once the eggplant has soaked up all the olive oil, add a splash of water and cover the pan until the eggplant is tender (see tip).
Then continue to cook uncovered, turning the slices occasionally. Season with salt and pepper.
Add a little olive oil to another pan and roast the pine nuts until they're golden brown. Finely chop and add the curly-leaf parsley. Be careful as this may spatter. Stir well and season with pepper and a little salt.
Remove the pan from heat, let it cool down a bit and add the shrimp.
Place the eggplant slices on a platter and arrange the shrimp and pine nuts over the top.

Tip: adding water to eggplant

Eggplant is sometimes a bit rubbery, even after it's cooked, unless you add lots and lots of olive oil. To avoid this, I pour in a splash of olive oil and cover the pan immediately. The steam in the pan speeds up the cooking process and makes the eggplant wonderfully soft. You can remove the lid after a couple of minutes.

Per serving: 26.7g P (21.2%) / 5.2g NetC (4.2%) / 41.9g F (74.6%)

Sauerkraut with bacon and sausage

Preparation time: 10 minutes – Cooking time: 15 minutes

3 ½ oz (100 g) bacon
3 ½ oz (100 g) plain sausage
3 ½ oz (100 g) chorizo sausage
14 oz (400 g) sauerkraut
mustard (unsweetened), optional

Cut the bacon into pieces. Cut some of the sausages also into pieces if you wish.
Put a little butter in a pan (the meat will also give off a lot of fat) and fry the bacon and sausages.
Drain the sauerkraut. Pour most of the fat from the sausage pan and add the sauerkraut. Don't let the sauerkraut cook, just heat it gently (see tip).
Serve with mustard if desired.

Tip: meat

I don't eat much meat, but when I do, I savor it to the fullest. I always choose quality meat, especially with sausages. That's why I always go to an organic butcher, so I know what's in them. The idea is that you take 5 ounces or 150 grams of meat per person, and this can be anything you like.
You'll see that the meat releases a lot of fat during the cooking process. I don't use all the fat but pour some of it off instead.

Tip: sauerkraut

Sauerkraut contains live bacteria (probiotics), which are ideal for your microbiome. That's why I don't cook the sauerkraut but heat it gently instead. Avoid pasteurized cabbage, as the process kills all those healthy probiotics.

Per serving: 33.2g P (22.8%) / 7.8g NetC (5.3%) / 46.6g F (71.9%)

This is a classic dish;
it's timeless and requires
very little preparation.

RECIPES

Extra

Not done with keto yet? You'll find extra recipes here. You can also switch recipes from the two-week meal plan with recipes from this part of the book. I've also included some delicious desserts in the back. But, if your goal is to lose weight, go easy on the desserts. It's also important that you can keep this up. Enjoy!

Creative breakfast eggs

Preparation time: 20 minutes – Cooking time: 20 minutes

Makes 6

Egg base

5 eggs
1 oz (30 g) cream

Filling

2 oz (60 g) broccoli florets
¾ oz (20 g) fresh herbs:
dill, chives, flat-leaf parsley ...
1 tomato

Garnish

1 slice of salmon
1 slice of ham
feta cheese

Extra: a muffin tin or silicone muffin pan

Very finely chop the broccoli florets; use only the florets, not the stem. Slice the tomato into quarters and remove the juice and seeds. Dice the flesh into pieces. Combine with the broccoli, add a tablespoon olive oil and season with salt and pepper.
Whisk the eggs together with the cream. Season with a little salt and pepper.
Finely chop the herbs.

Preheat the oven to 350 °F (180 °C).
Divide the vegetables over all six muffin cups. Divide the feta cheese evenly between two cups, the salmon between another two cups, and the ham between the final 2 cups. Sprinkle the fresh herbs over the top. Finish with some feta, salmon, and ham in the corresponding muffin cups.
Pour the egg mixture into the cups.
Bake in the oven for about 20 minutes or until the egg has set.

Note: salmon, ham and feta cheese

I've calculated 2 muffins per person. You can, of course, choose just salmon or just cheese or meat, ideal for when you want to make 12 at a time (so double this recipe). Then you'll have breakfast for the coming 3 days. One day salmon, the other day ham and a third day cheese. The fun thing is, it invites you to be creative.

Per muffin with 1 ½ oz (40 g) salmon: 15.5g P (34.2%) / 1.3g NetC (2.8%) / 12.7g F (63%)
Per muffin with 1 ½ oz (40 g) ham: 14.9g P (40%) / 1.6g NetC (4%) / 9.3g F (56%)
Per muffin with 1 ½ oz (40 g) feta cheese: 12.3g P (22.6%) / 1.9g NetC (3.7%) / 17.8g F (73.7%)

Fill them up
with meat, cheese
or salmon ...

Omelet surprise with sautéed mushrooms and jumbo shrimp

Preparation time: 15 minutes – Cooking time: 15 minutes

4 eggs
7 oz (200 g) mushrooms
3 ½ oz (100 g) peeled jumbo shrimp
1 teaspoon red curry paste
handful of flat-leaf parsley

Coarsely chop the mushrooms and sauté them in olive oil or butter. Season with salt and pepper. Meanwhile, dice and add the jumbo shrimp. Once they're done, add a teaspoonful of red curry paste and some flat-leaf parsley. Continue to cook.

Beat together 2 eggs, season with salt and pepper and fry them to make a thin omelet. Let cook a little longer. Don't turn the omelet over. As soon as the omelet has set on the top, place half the filling on the omelet and fold both sides in on top of the filling. Make the second omelet in the same way with the other 2 eggs and the leftover filling.

Per serving: 22g P (19%) / 1.4g NetC (1.3%) / 41.1g F (79.7%)

The combination
of shrimp,
red curry paste,
and mushrooms
in an omelet
is heavenly.

Breakfast with strawberries and warm cream

Preparation time: 5 minutes – Cooking time: 5 minutes

- 3 ½ oz (100 g) strawberries
- 10 ½ oz (300 g) cream
- a teaspoonful (5 g) ground roasted sesame seeds (garnish, optional)
- 1 g (a scant ½ teaspoonful) agar-agar

This breakfast tastes best when eaten lukewarm as a delicious, creamy porridge.

Dice the strawberries and cook them in 1 tablespoon olive oil. Put the cream in a small saucepan, mix in the agar-agar and heat. Let the mixture cook, stirring constantly. Remove the pan from heat and mix three quarters of the strawberries into the cream. Divide the strawberry cream over two bowls. Let it cool and then garnish with the remaining strawberries and some ground sesame seeds.
Serve slightly warm.

Tip: agar-agar

Agar-agar is a substance derived from algae which releases its jelly-like structure when heated. It's an easy, practical, and vegetarian substitute for gelatin. It's not hard to find, particularly in health food stores. Note: don't use too much as it also takes away some of the flavor. 1 gram is enough for this recipe. The more it cools, the thicker the cream will be.

Tip: strawberries

Strawberries are probably the most keto-friendly of the berries, as they contain about 5 grams net carbs per 100 grams.
I've used 3 ½ ounces, or 100 grams in this recipe. That's the amount you see portrayed in the bowl on the photo. It's not much, but it's enough to bring out that delicious strawberry flavor, even with keto.

Per serving: 4.1g P (2.5%) / 7g NetC (4.4%) / 66.3g F (93.1%)

Zucchini rolls with smoked salmon and nori

Preparation time: 20 minutes – Cooking time: 15 minutes

Makes about 10 rolls
1 zucchini
2 slices smoked salmon
2 sheets nori seaweed

Preheat the oven to 350 °F (180 °C).
With a vegetable peeler, slice thin strips lengthways from the zucchini. Pick out the 10 nicest slices; you can work the rest of the zucchini slices into a salad. Arrange the slices next to each other, rub them in with olive oil and season with pepper.
You don't need to add salt; the smoked salmon is salty enough.
Cut the nori sheets into long strips. Place a nori strip and a piece of salmon on each zucchini slice. Roll the slice up and place the appetizers in a baking dish. Bake in the oven for about 15 minutes. Serve with a skewer or on a small plate.

A delicious snack, and so very keto. :-)

Per roll: 2.3g P (24.3%) / 0.4g NetC (5.4%) / 2.9g F (70.3%)

Goat's cheese with roasted pumpkin seeds

Preparation time: 5 minutes – Cooking time: 7 minutes

Serves 6

6 oz (180 g) creamy goat cheese
1 ¾ oz (50 g) pumpkin seeds (see tip)

Preheat the oven to 350 °F (180 °C).
Sprinkle the pumpkin seeds into a baking dish and bake them in the oven for about 7 minutes or until they start to change color and puff up (see tip). Remove them from the oven and season with black pepper and fleur de sel.
Shape the goat cheese into balls or quenelles by turning the cheese between two spoons (just like ice cream) and coat them with the pumpkin seeds.

Tip: roasting pumpkin seeds

Note that pumpkin seeds turn just as brown as pine nuts when you roast them. They're ready when they start to puff up, and you'll sometimes hear them burst. Make sure you don't burn them. Try them!
This is great example of how much the carb charts differ from each other: for pumpkin seeds, you'll find values ranging from 2.8 grams to 15.2 grams carbs per 100 grams.

Roasted pumpkin seeds taste so good! And they fit perfectly into a keto cure as long as you don't eat too many of them.

Per piece: 7.3g P (22.5%) / 1.2g NetC (3.9%) / 10.6g F (73.6%)

Zucchini with raw ham

Preparation time: 15 minutes – Cooking time: 15 minutes

Makes 8

2 zucchini
(a little over 1 lb/500 g)
16 slices raw ham
(prosciutto crudo or other smoked ham ...)
lemon
dried thyme

Preheat the oven to 350 °F (180 °C).
Slice the zucchini lengthways into quarters. Remove the seeds.
Put the zucchini sticks in a baking dish. Drizzle with a generous amount of olive oil (about 4 tablespoons) and season with plenty of thyme, a generous grind of black pepper and a little salt.
Don't use too much salt; the ham is already salty. Rub the oil and herbs into the zucchini so they're evenly coated all over.
Wrap two slices of ham around each zucchini stick.
Bake the zucchini 10 to 15 minutes on a grill or broil in the oven.
Place half a lemon with the cut side down on the grill until it starts to change color.
Serve immediately.

Per piece: 9.1g P (31.3%) / 0.5g NetC (1.7%) / 8.5g F (67%)

Ideal for when
you're not feeling
particularly hungry
or as a first course.

Savoy cabbage rolls with smoked trout and almonds

Preparation time: 30 minutes – Cooking time: 15 minutes

Makes about 6 rolls

- 6 Savoy cabbage leaves (tough leaf stems removed, about 10 ½ oz/300 g)
- 10 ½ oz (300 g) smoked trout fillets
- 1 shallot
- small handful unpeeled almonds (¾ oz/20 g + ⅓ oz/10 g extra)
- 3 sprigs tarragon (or thyme), leaves removed from the stems
- juice of ½ lemon

Preheat the oven to 350 °F (180 °C).

Thoroughly rinse the Savoy cabbage leaves and cut out the tough leaf stems. Drain off the excess water and pat them dry with a tea towel or kitchen towels.

Heat a splash of olive oil in a large frying pan and sauté the cabbage leaves one by one until browned on both sides.

Season with salt and pepper and set aside to cool on a platter.

Finely chop the shallot and tarragon.

Lightly roast the almonds for about 10 minutes in the oven and coarsely chop them.

Mash the trout fillets with a fork and stir in the shallot, ¾ ounces (20 grams) of the chopped almonds and two sprigs of the tarragon (or thyme). Add a splash of olive oil and the lemon juice. Season with black pepper (you don't need salt; the trout is salty enough).

Spread the cabbage leaves out on a cutting board. Spoon some of the trout filling onto the leaves and roll them up tightly.

Diagonally slice the cabbage rolls into servings and arrange them on a serving dish. Sprinkle the remaining almonds and tarragon (thyme) over the top and drizzle with a few drops of olive oil.

Per piece: 12.8g P (32.9%) / 2.8g NetC (7.1%) / 10.3g F (60%)

A delightfully harmonious
combination of flavors.

Chicken liver pâté with avocado and walnuts

Preparation time: 10 minutes – Cooking time: 15 minutes

This is a delicious and such an incredibly healthy recipe. Promise me you'll give it a chance and try it at least once.

9 oz (250 g) chicken livers (ideally organic)
5 oz (150 g) pork belly, in pieces
1 ripe avocado
1 medium-sized onion (2 ½ oz/70 g)
1 clove of garlic
1 tbsp sherry vinegar
1 ½ oz (40 g) walnuts
5 sprigs thyme (optional)

Coarsely chop half the walnuts. Fry the pork belly pieces in a little olive oil (pork belly releases quite a bit of fat) until they're cooked through. Add the walnuts during the final minute of cooking. Set the pork belly and walnut mixture aside once it's cooked.
Mince the onion and garlic and sauté gently in olive oil. Make sure they don't turn brown.
Meanwhile, clean the chicken livers; remove the fat, any white threads and anything else that doesn't look appetizing. Slice the livers into ¾-inch (2 cm) pieces. Add them to the onion and let everything simmer for another 4 or 5 minutes, stirring constantly. Ideally, the livers should still be light pink on the inside; overcooked liver tends to have a grainy texture. Add a splash of sherry vinegar and the leaves from the thyme sprigs if desired. Let the mixture simmer a little longer.
Put the chicken liver in a food processor and add the avocado. Blend until you have a smooth, creamy paste. Season with salt and pepper.
Put everything in a bowl and stir in the fried pork belly and walnuts. Spoon everything into an attractive dish and garnish with the remaining walnuts. Let the pâté firm up in the fridge for at least 15 minutes before serving.
This pâté will keep for up to three days in the refrigerator.

Tip: why liver?
Organ meat has a high concentration of healthy nutrients, including vitamins, minerals and fatty acids. Liver in particular scores high on this scale; some even refer to it as a superfood. In the wild, predators usually pick out the liver, kidneys and heart first; they only get round to the muscle tissue if they're still hungry. We also see this in traditional indigenous communities, where organ meat is held in high regard.

For 1/10 of this recipe: 9.3g P (22.2%) / 1.7g NetC (4.1%) / 14g F (73.7%)

Seed and nut crackers with mackerel rillette

Preparation time: 15 minutes – Cooking time: 15 minutes

1 ¾ oz (50 g) flaxseed
1 ¾ oz (50 g) hazelnuts
1 egg white

For the mackerel rillette
3 ½ oz (100 g) smoked mackerel fillet
1 shallot
2 spring onions

Preheat the oven to 350 °F (180 °C).
Grind the nuts down to a powder and combine with the flaxseed and egg white. Season with salt and pepper. Roll out into a thin layer between two sheets of baking parchment.
Remove the top sheet of parchment paper and bake for 10 minutes.
Turn the cracker over and cook for another 5 minutes.
Keep an eye on the baking process, as every oven is different.
Blend the mackerel fillets with the shallot, spring onions and salt and pepper to a thick paste.
Mackerel is creamy in itself and so it will be easy to blend.
A shallot and a spring onion are enough for a delicious cracker.

Tip: more crackers
Feel free to make more crackers; they will keep up to 3 days at room temperature. You can also freeze them for later; gently defrost them and pop them briefly in the oven to make them light and crispy again.

Per cracker: 5.4g P (19.1%) / 1g NetC (3.5%) / 9.9g F (77.4%)

Ham rolls with mushroom paste

Preparation time: 15 minutes – Cooking time: 15 minutes

9 oz (250 g) cremini or baby bella mushrooms
2 shallots
2 cloves of garlic
2 tablespoons mascarpone
12 slices dry-cured ham

A wonderful treat: attractive and delicious!

Preheat the oven to 350 °F (180 °C).
Mince the mushrooms into very small pieces and sauté them in a pan with 3 tablespoons olive oil.
Finely chop and add the shallots and garlic.
Season with salt and pepper.
Let the mixture cook for about 7 minutes until you start smelling the aroma of cooked mushrooms. Remove from the heat and stir in the mascarpone. Take a slice of ham, spoon a large tablespoonful of mushroom paste into the middle and roll up. Place the roll in a baking dish; do the same with the rest of the ham slices and mushroom paste.
Put the baking dish in the oven for 15 minutes.
These appetizers are so tasty and easy to serve.

Tip: serve separately
The mushroom paste is very rich in flavor. You can serve it on its own with meat or fish.

Per roll: 5.2g P (21.9%) / 0.9g NetC (4.2%) / 7.9g F (73.9%)

You can make these appetizers separately if you wish. I've doubled the portions for the photos. Ideal for when you have guests over.

Three recipes in one:

Cauliflower and eggplant hummus with sesame seed crackers

Sesame seed crackers

Preparation time: 10 minutes – Cooking time: 15 minutes

Makes about 10 crackers

- 1 ¾ oz (50 g) sesame seeds
- 1 ¾ oz (50 g) flaxseed
- 1 oz (30 g) finely grated Parmesan cheese
- 1 egg white

Extra: baking parchment

These are "passe-partout" crackers ... They'll go with anything.

Preheat the oven to 350 °F (180 °C).

Coarsely ground the flaxseed. Combine the rest of the ingredients and add 3 tablespoons water to the mixture.

Season with some salt and pepper.

Place the mixture between 2 sheets of baking parchment and roll out to a thickness of 2 mm (very thin). (If you don't have a rolling pin, try using a bottle instead.)

Remove the top sheet of parchment paper. Take a large knife and press down to make squares (see tip).

Bake in the oven for 10 minutes. Remove the bottom sheet of parchment paper and put the crackers back in the oven for 5 to 10 minutes with the bottom facing up until lightly browned and crispy.

Tip: cutting the dough into squares

Take a large knife and press the knife into the seeds. Don't cut because the seeds will stick to the knife. Scoring them is enough, so they will break nice and evenly once they're baked. Another option is to avoid scoring the dough altogether and break the sheet afterwards into random pieces.

Per cracker (1/10 recipe): 3.7g P (23.1%) / 0.5g NetC (3.1%) / 5.3g F (73.8%)

Cauliflower hummus

Preparation time: 10 minutes – Cooking time: 30 minutes

7 oz (200 g) cauliflower
1 tablespoon tahini (sesame paste) (30 g)
1 teaspoon ground cumin
1 clove of garlic

Preheat the oven to 350 °F (180 °C).
Break the florets away from the cauliflower and cook them for 2 to 3 minutes in salted water.
Drain off the water and arrange the florets on a baking sheet.
Add the whole garlic clove to the cauliflower. Drizzle plenty of olive oil (¾ oz/20 g) over the top and roast in the oven for 20 to 30 minutes or until the cauliflower florets start to brown.
Combine the florets with the roasted garlic, tahini, 2 tablespoons olive oil, some pepper, salt and cumin.

The flavor, color and texture will be just the way hummus should be: absolutely delicious.

1 cracker + ¾ oz/20 g cauliflower hummus: 4.6g P (17%) / 1g NetC (3.8%) / 9.3g F (79.2%)

Eggplant hummus

Preparation time: 5 minutes – Cooking time: 30 minutes

1 small eggplant (7 oz/200 g)
3 small vine tomatoes (1 ¼ oz/40 g)
1 clove of garlic

For the garnish
paprika powder
flat-leaf parsley

I love cooked eggplant. :-)

Preheat the oven to 350 °F (180 °C).
Prick the eggplant in a couple of places with a fork and put it in the oven together with the garlic clove and the tomatoes. Bake for about 30 minutes.
Slice the cooked eggplant in half lengthways and spoon out the flesh. Put the flesh together with the cooked garlic in a blender or a food processor. Add 2 to 3 tablespoons olive oil, season with salt and pepper and blend to a smooth paste.

Tip: if you want to make both types of hummus, put everything together in the oven
I put both the cauliflower florets and the eggplant, garlic and tomatoes together in the oven on one baking sheet. The tomatoes are actually done after 15 minutes, but they taste even better if you leave them in for 30 minutes. And it doesn't get any easier than this: everything in one batch. I bake the crackers separately, though.

Serving
Spoon the cauliflower hummus onto the bottom of the plate. Make a well in the middle of the hummus with the back of a spoon. Spoon the eggplant hummus into the well. Arrange the tomatoes on top and garnish with a little sweet paprika powder and some finely chopped flat-leaf parsley. Drizzle a little olive oil over the top.
Enjoy these delicious vegetables. Serve with the crackers.

1 cracker + ¾ oz/20 g eggplant hummus: 3.9g P (18.2%) / 1g NetC (4.5%) / 7.5g F (77.3%)

Zucchini with tomatoes and feta

Preparation time: 10 minutes – Cooking time: 20 minutes

2 small zucchini (14 oz/400 g)
2 tomatoes (7 oz/200 g)
1 packet feta cheese
(7 oz/200 g)
dried thyme
handful roasted hazelnuts
(1 oz/ 30 g)

Preheat the oven to 350 °F (180 °C).
Slice the zucchini into thin strips with a vegetable peeler.
Put them in a baking dish.
Slice the tomatoes into wedges and remove the hard, white core.
Add them to the sliced zucchini. Crumble three quarters of the feta over the vegetables, drizzle with plenty of olive oil and season with pepper, thyme and a little salt. Toss together well until everything is coated with the feta-oil mixture. Crumble the rest of the feta on top and garnish with the hazelnuts.
Bake in the oven for 20 minutes.

Just 10 minutes of work and worth every minute!

Per serving: 20.8g P (15.4%) / 7.3g NetC (5.4%) / 47.5g F (79.2%)

A simple and fun
keto recipe.

Tomato and mozzarella stuffed portobello

Preparation time: 7 minutes – Cooking time: 20 minutes

- 2 large portobello mushrooms (a little over 1 lb/500 g)
- 2 tomatoes (7 oz/200 g)
- 1 bunch fresh basil (¾ oz/20 g)
- 2 balls mozzarella cheese
- sweet paprika powder (optional)

Preheat the oven to 350 °F (180 °C).
Quarter the tomatoes; you can leave the skin on.
Remove the juice and seeds and dice the flesh. Combine the diced tomato with 3 tablespoons olive oil and season with salt and pepper. Finely chop the basil and stir it into the diced tomato.
Coat the inside and outside of the portobellos with olive oil.
The mushrooms will instantly soak up the oil. Season with pepper and a little salt. Dice the mozzarella.
First fill the portobellos with the tomato mixture, right up to the top. Place the mozzarella in the middle and sprinkle a little paprika powder on top.
Bake in the oven for about 30 minutes.

Tip: portobello mushrooms

A portobello is actually just a large cremini or baby bella mushroom. The caps can reach a diameter of up to 4 to 5 inches, ideal for stuffing. If you can't find large portobello mushrooms, use smaller mushroom varieties. They are exceptionally low in carbs (0.6 g C/100 g), so you're allowed to eat plenty of them.

Per serving: 31.8g P (20.9%) / 6.2g NetC (4.1%) / 50.6g F (75%)

Raw salmon with avocado

Preparation time: 12 minutes – Cooking time: none

slices raw (or smoked) salmon, about 5 oz/150 g per person
1 avocado
1 oz (30 g) pistachios
a handful fresh herbs (chives, basil, coriander ...)
1 jar salmon roe (1 ¾ oz/50 g)
1 shallot
cider vinegar

Spoon the flesh from the avocado and dice into pieces.
Finely chop the pistachios.
Finely chop the herbs and slice the shallot into rings.
Put the avocado, nuts (keep some aside for the garnish), herbs and shallot in a bowl, add a small splash of cider vinegar and season with salt and pepper. Mix everything together. Arrange the salmon slices over two plates and divide the avocado mixture over the top. Spoon some salmon roe over the plates and garnish with the remaining pistachio crumble.

Tip: keto
This is the keto version of a recipe from my book *Echt Eten* ('Real Food'). We use cider vinegar here instead of white balsamic vinegar and are a little more sparing with the pistachios: 1 oz (30 g) instead of 2 oz (60 g. pistachios contain about 9 grams C per 100 grams).

Per serving: 37.7g P (23.6%) / 7.7g NetC (4.8%) / 51g F (71.6%)

Zucchini noodles with tomato, mushrooms and cheese sauce

Preparation time: 10 minutes – Cooking time: 10 minutes

2 or 3 zucchini (enough for about 14 oz/400 g zucchini noodles)
2 medium-sized tomatoes (7 oz/200 g)
9 oz (250 g) cremini or baby bella mushrooms

For the sauce
3 ½ fl oz (100 ml) full-fat cream
3 ½ oz (100 g) grated Parmesan cheese
handful shaved Parmesan cheese (about 1 oz/30 g)

Slice the zucchini into long strips with a serrated vegetable peeler. Put them in a bowl and toss them in a little olive oil. Set aside so they can marinate and soften.
Remove the seeds from the tomatoes and dice the flesh.
Dice the mushrooms and fry them in a pan with some olive oil. Season with salt and pepper.
Heat the cream in a separate saucepan together with the Parmesan cheese until you have a thick, creamy sauce. Season with salt and pepper.
Mix the vegetables together but keep some diced tomato and mushrooms aside for the garnish. Carefully stir the vegetables into the cheese sauce and top with the leftover diced tomatoes and mushrooms. Garnish with the Parmesan shavings.

A plate full of healthy vegetables and brimming with delicious, rich flavor.

Per serving: 33.2g P (19%) / 8.2g NetC (4.7%) / 59.5g F (76.3%)

Homemade steak tartare spread

Preparation time: 15 minutes – Cooking time: none

For the steak tartare
10 ½ oz (300 g) minced beef tenderloin (see tip)
2 shallots
2 egg yolks
1 tablespoon mustard
2 tablespoons light soy sauce
a few drops of Tabasco sauce
2 tablespoons capers
⅓ oz (10 g) curly-leaf parsley
2 cherry tomatoes (garnish)

For the salad
lettuce
2 tomatoes
flat-leaf parsley

Finely chop the shallots and the curly-leaf parsley.
Put the meat in a bowl and add the egg yolks, shallot, parsley, capers, mustard, soy sauce, 1 tablespoon olive oil and a little tabasco to taste. Season with pepper. Be careful with using salt, because soy sauce is already salty. Combine thoroughly.
For the salad, arrange some lettuce leaves in two bowls.
Slice the tomatoes into wedges. Coarsely chop some flat-leaf parsley and add to the bowls. Season with salt and pepper.
Drizzle 2 to 3 tablespoons olive oil over each salad.
Divide the tartare over the plates and press it into shape with a fork.
Garnish with some flat-leaf parsley. Slice the cherry tomatoes into fan shapes and arrange them on the tartare.

Tip: meat
You can use different types of meat to make steak tartare spread. Visit your local butcher and ask him for meat for steak tartare. If he can't grind it for you, you'll have to chop it up at home. :-) The meat must be fresh and pure, though.

Tip: steak tartare spread
This is a typical Belgian recipe, the creation of Brussels native Joseph Niels. It was his best take on steak tartare, which he served in his restaurant, Canterbury. Whether this is the original recipe, I don't know, but this version is delicious – and keto-proof.

Per serving: 38.2g P (32.6%) / 9.6g NetC (8.1%) / 30.9g F (59.3%)

Belgian culinary
history on your plate.
Make sure that the meat
is fresh and pure.

Zucchini noodles with a tomato-cheese sauce and macadamia crumble

Preparation time: 15 minutes – Cooking time: 10 minutes

10 ½ oz (300 g) zucchini noodles
5 oz (150 g) cream
3 ½ (100 g) grated Emmental cheese
1 large tomato

For the crumble
¾ oz (20 g) macadamia nuts
¾ oz (20 g) Parmesan cheese
¾ oz (20 g) fresh basil

A keto vegetable dish that tastes even better than the original. :-) Mouth-watering!

If you're making fresh zucchini noodles, do them first (see tip).

Crumble

Put the nuts, Parmesan cheese and basil leaves in a food processor and blend to a crumble. Put the crumble in a jar and set aside.

Quarter the tomatoes and remove the seeds and juice. You should have about 3 ½ oz (100 grams) tomato left. Dice the flesh and sauté it for a couple of minutes in olive oil. Add the cream and the cheese and stir until the cheese has fully melted into the cream. If you prefer a slightly runnier sauce, add a little water. Season with salt and pepper.
Add the drained zucchini noodles and stir them into the sauce. Divide the vegetables over the plates and serve with the macadamia crumble.

Tip: zucchini noodles

If you're making your own zucchini noodles, prepare them first. Make sure you have about 10 ½ oz (300 g) zucchini noodles. Put them in a colander and toss them with a little salt. Leave them to drain while you prepare the rest of the dish. Be careful with the salt: if you use a lot of salt with the noodles, don't add any more salt to the sauce.

Per serving: 22.9g P (13.1%) / 6.1g NetC (3.5%) / 64.9g F (83.4%)

Caesar salad with kale

Preparation time: 10 minutes – Cooking time: 7 minutes

10 ½ oz (300 g) chicken breasts
3 ½ oz (100 g) kale (see tip)

For the sauce
2 ½ oz (70 g) cream
1 to 2 tablespoons mustard (to taste)
¾ oz (20 g) roasted sesame seeds

Dice the chicken into small pieces and brown them in a little butter. Season with salt and pepper.
Thoroughly rinse the kale. Tear the thick veins from the kale leaves and divide the leaves over the plates. You will discover that 1 ½ oz (40 grams) per person should be enough. Arrange the chicken pieces on top.
Combine the cream and the mustard and season with salt and pepper.
Grind the roasted sesame seeds down to a coarse powder.
Divide the sauce over the plates and sprinkle the roasted sesame seeds over the top.

Tip: kale
Consuming enough fiber is always a challenge with a ketogenic diet. That's why The Keto Cure contains plenty of vegetables, but raw vegetables are both healthy and a good source of fiber. That's why I suggest using raw kale for this lunch recipe. If you don't like raw kale or find it's too tough, you can replace it with another type of lettuce.

Tip: Caesar salad
Caesar salad has nothing to do with the Roman emperor, Julius Caesar; it was invented by the Italian chef Caesar Cardini. This dish is a variation on this classic salad. Technically, this dish requires an egg, but I think a ketogenic diet has more than its fair share of eggs already. :-)

Per serving: 40.5g P (32.8%) / 3.3g NetC (2.6%) / 35.4g F (64.6%)

The sauce with the roasted sesame seeds is a delicious combination!

An exquisite keto dish.

Haddock with fried seeds and nuts, asparagus and foamy mayonnaise

Preparation time: 20 minutes – Cooking time: 20 minutes

2 haddock fillets
1 oz (30 g) mixed seeds and nuts (pumpkin seeds, hazelnuts ...)
12 white asparagus

For the foamy mayonnaise
2 eggs
olive oil (or peanut oil for a more neutral flavor)
juice of ½ lemon
mustard

Preheat the oven to 350 °F (180 °C).
Pour a splash of olive oil in a baking dish, coat the fish with the oil and season with salt and pepper. Bake in the oven for about 15 minutes. Peel the asparagus and cook them as desired (I like them al dente) in water with a generous splash of olive oil.
Pour some olive oil in a pan and roast the seeds and nuts until light golden brown. Season with salt and pepper.

Foamy mayonnaise:
Separate the eggs into yolks and whites and put the egg whites in a bowl.
We'll use the egg yolks to make a normal mayonnaise first.
Put them in blender, add a tablespoonful olive oil and a heaped tablespoonful mustard and blend for a couple of seconds. Add the oil in a steady stream as you continue to mix. Add as much oil as you need to get the desired amount. Add a little lemon juice, mustard, salt and pepper to taste.
Beat the egg whites until peaks form. Take 5 tablespoons mayonnaise and fold in 3 to 4 tablespoons of the beaten egg whites to get a frothy mayonnaise. Arrange the asparagus on the plates, place the fish on top and spoon the roasted seeds and nuts over the fish. Garnish with the foamy mayonnaise.

What is foamy mayonnaise?
That's easy: it's just normal mayonnaise with frothy beaten egg whites mixed in. Add the egg whites at the very last minute, so the foamy mayonnaise stays nice and firm.

Per serving: 40.4g P (29.3%) / 6g NetC (4.4%) / 40.7g P (66.3%)

Salmon with cauliflower rice and ras-el-hanout

Preparation time: 5 minutes – Cooking time: 10 minutes

2 salmon fillets, with skin
½ head of cauliflower (approx. 10 ½ or 300 g)
handful of hazelnuts (1 oz/ 30 g)
2 spring onions, finely chopped
ras-el-hanout

Grate the cauliflower to make cauliflower rice.
Cook the cauliflower and hazelnuts in plenty of olive oil, stirring regularly.
In a separate pan, sear the salmon on both sides, making sure that the inside stays pink. Season with salt and pepper.
When the cauliflower is almost tender, stir in 2 teaspoons ras-el-hanout, plenty of black pepper and a little salt. Add another splash of olive oil and keep stirring until everything is cooked through.
Spoon the cauliflower rice onto a plate and place the salmon on top.
Garnish with the finely chopped spring onions.

Deliciously creamy spiced cauliflower.

Per serving: 32.7g P (19%) / 5.5g NetC (3.2%) / 59.4g F (77.8%)

Shrimp and zucchini noodles in a curried coconut sauce

Preparation time: 6 minutes – Cooking time: 10 minutes

12 frozen jumbo shrimp (14 oz/400 g)
1 to 2 tablespoons green curry paste (to taste)
2 zucchini (or 10 ½ oz/ 300 g zucchini noodles)
6 lime leaves
juice of ½ lime
9 oz (250 ml) coconut milk
2 cloves of garlic

Bring the coconut milk to a boil together with the lime leaves, lime juice, crushed garlic and 1 to 2 tablespoons curry paste to taste.
Slice the zucchini into thin strips (use only the outer part; throw away the seeds or use them in soup).
Add the frozen shrimp to the coconut milk. Once the shrimp are cooked through, add the zucchini noodles. Simmer 1 more minute.
Divide the shrimp and noodles over the plates and garnish with black pepper.

A dish that will make you happy! Not much work, wonderful to look at and oh, so delicious!

Per serving: 27g P (30.5%) / 6g NetC (6.8%) / 24.7g F (62.7%)

Minced lamb with herbed yogurt sauce

Preparation time: 25 minutes – Cooking time: 10 minutes

10 ½ oz (300 g) minced lamb
dried thyme and rosemary

For the yogurt sauce
4 ½ oz (125 g) full-fat yogurt
10 ½ oz (300 g) cucumber
1 clove of garlic
fresh mint

For the salad
lettuce
1 tomato

Extra: long skewers

Slice the cucumber in half lengthways and scrape out the seeds and moisture with a teaspoon. Dice the flesh into large pieces. Finely chop the garlic and put it together with the cucumber in a bowl. Season with some salt and mix. Set aside for a moment.
Season the minced lamb with some dried (or fresh) thyme, rosemary, pepper and salt. Knead the herbs into the meat. Divide the lamb into six piles and shape them around the skewers. Flatten them slightly so they're easier to fry. Fry the lamb skewers on both sides in butter (¾ oz/ 20 g).
Take a clean tea towel or muslin cloth and spoon the chopped cucumber into the towel. Wring as much of the moisture out of the cucumber as you can. Put the cucumber in a bowl and combine with the yogurt. Finely chop some fresh mint and mix this into the yogurt.
Divide the lettuce over the plates. Arrange some tomato slices on the lettuce. Season with salt and pepper and drizzle some olive oil over the top. Divide the yogurt sauce over two bowls and arrange the meat next to the sauce on the plate. Garnish with some extra finely chopped mint (or any fresh herbs you want).

Tip: lamb
I personally love lamb, but I know not everyone likes lamb as much as I do. You can use another type of minced meat for this dish. Whatever you use, make sure you season the meat to give it a Mediterranean touch.

Per serving: 29.5g P (16.5%) / 9g NetC (5.1%) / 62.2g F (78.4%)

A delightfully refreshing
and summery dish.

Seasoned meatballs in a curry sauce with endive

Preparation time: 15 minutes – Cooking time: 15 minutes

10 ½ oz (300 g) minced chicken
3 heads of endive
(a little over 1 lb/500 g)
2 tablespoons green curry paste
3 ½ oz (100 g) coconut milk
a sprinkling of flaked almonds(½ oz/15 g)
1 teaspoon ras-el-hanout

Combine the chicken mince with the ras-el-hanout, salt and pepper. Knead well and shape into 8 to 10 balls. Cook them in plenty of butter (¾ oz/20 g).
Slice the endive into strips and cook them in ¾ oz (20 g) butter. Season with salt and pepper. As soon as the endive is tender, add the coconut milk and stir in the green curry paste.
Serve the endive and the sauce in deep dishes, arrange the cooked chicken meatballs in the sauce and sprinkle the flaked almonds on top.
Delicious!

Tip: endive
Endive pairs really well with a curry sauce. Endive used to taste bitter, but because most people don't like its bitter taste, you'll find less pronounced varieties in the supermarkets these days. Endive is also an exceptionally keto-friendly vegetable: it contains few carbs, between 1 and 2 grams per 100 grams.

Per serving: 33.9g P (21.1%) / 9g NetC (5.6%) / 52.5g F (73.3%)

Endive pairs really well with curry.

The combination of leek and endive is heavenly.

Fried haloumi with endive and leek

Preparation time: 15 minutes – Cooking time: 15 minutes

1 packet halloumi cheese
3 heads of endive
(about 12 oz/350 g)
7 to 8-inch (20-cm) leek
(about 5 oz/150 g) (see tip)
1 clove of garlic
splash of cream (1 oz/30 g)
a few sprigs of thyme

Slice the leek and endive into rings and sauté them in plenty of butter (¾ ounce/ 20 grams). Finely chop the garlic, remove the thyme leaves from the stem, and add to the vegetables.
Season with salt and pepper. Add the cream as soon as the vegetables are tender.
Slice the halloumi. The halloumi may crumble as you slice it, but don't worry, it'll give you all sorts of fun shapes. Fry the halloumi slices in a pan with a little fat until they start to change color. Turn them over. You don't need to season them, a couple of twists of the black pepper mill at most.
Place the vegetables in a deep dish, arrange the halloumi on top and garnish with some fried thyme sprigs.

Tip: leek

Leek is not the most keto-friendly vegetable: it contains about 9 grams carbs per 100 grams. That's the reason why this dish contains more carbs than some of my other recipes. But if you don't eat too much of it and you combine it with endive, which contains very few carbs, you should be okay. And the combination is fabulous.
Leek contains inulin, a type of prebiotic: food for your gut bacteria.

Per serving: 30.2g P (19.6%) / 12.9g NetC (8.4%) / 49.3g F (72%)

Vegetable curry with pecans

Preparation time: 15 minutes – Cooking time: 20 minutes

7 oz (200 g) cauliflower
7 oz (200 g) cremini or baby bella mushrooms
7 oz (200 g) green asparagus
7 oz (200 g) coconut milk
1 ½ oz (50 g) pecans
¾ oz (20 g) red curry paste

Put the cauliflower florets in a pan together with a splash of water and 2 tablespoons olive oil. Cover the pan and cook/steam the cauliflower until tender.
Cut the mushrooms into large pieces and sauté them in 3 tablespoons olive oil. Season with salt and pepper. Slice away the hard bottom of the asparagus stalks. Slice the asparagus in half and add them to the mushrooms. Continue to stir-fry the vegetables over medium heat. Finally, add the pecans. Season with salt and pepper.
Stir the red curry paste into the cold coconut milk (note: add a tablespoonful at a time and keep tasting so the dish doesn't become too spicy).
Drain any leftover water from the cauliflower, return the pan to the heat and add the curried cream. Warm everything through.
Carefully stir the cauliflower into the curried cream. Divide the cauliflower curry over two plates and arrange the other vegetables next to it.

A scrumptious vegan dish, bursting with flavor.

Per serving: 8.1g P (5%) / 8.9g NetC (5.6%) / 63.3g F (89.4%)

Blackberry ice cream

Preparation time: 5 minutes – Cooking time: 20 minutes in the freezer

5 oz (150 g) blackberries (+ some extra to garnish, if desired)
3 ½ oz (100 g) cream
1 oz (30 g) pistachios

Put the blackberries in the freezer for about 30 minutes until they're completely frozen. Coarsely chop the pistachios. Blend the frozen blackberries together with the cream in a sturdy blender to make a thick creamy paste. Add more cream if the ice cream is too grainy.
Spoon the ice cream into balls and serve immediately.
Garnish with the pistachio crumble.

Tip: instant blackberry ice cream
I always have a container of blackberries sitting around in the freezer when they're in season, so I can instantly make delicious blackberry ice cream whenever I feel like it.

Per serving: 4.9g P (6.7%) / 8g NetC (10.7%) / 27.4g F (82.6%)

An ideal keto dessert,
pure and natural!

Fruit is not the first thing that comes to mind when you think of a ketogenic diet. And when we do, we often think only of berries; but peaches also contain relatively few carbs: 7 g C/100 g They fit perfectly into a keto cure as long as you don't eat too many of them.

Oven-baked peaches with mascarpone and nut paste

Preparation time: 6 minutes – Cooking time: 20 minutes

2 peaches (7 oz/200 g)
7 oz (200 g) mascarpone
2 teaspoons nut paste
2 tablespoons flaked almonds (½ oz/15 g)

Preheat the oven to 350 °F (180 °C).
Quarter the peaches and put them in a small baking dish. Beat the mascarpone with a fork until smooth, add the nut paste and stir a couple of times with the back of a spoon. Don't mix the nut paste and mascarpone too thoroughly; we still want to keep some white lumps in the mixture. Divide the mascarpone mixture over the peaches and sprinkle some flaked almonds over the top.
Bake in the oven for 15 to 20 minutes.

Tip: keto
This is the keto version of a recipe from *Echt Eten* ('Real food') with more mascarpone and smaller peaches. One small peach weighs about 100 grams and contains about 7 grams of carbs. That's quite a few, but just about okay. Combine this breakfast with a lunch or dinner that has fewer carbs.
If you have trouble reaching ketosis, you should probably choose a different breakfast with fewer carbs.

Per serving: 10.5g P (7.3%) / 11.7g NetC (8.2%) / 53.7g F (84.4%)

Chocolate fudge with nut paste

Preparation time: 10 minutes – Cooking time: 20 minutes

1 oz (30 g) coconut milk
1 oz (30 g) Philadelphia plain cream cheese
1 egg
1 ½ tablespoon cocoa powder
1 tablespoon erythritol (to taste)
2 teaspoons cold nut paste (see tip)

Extra: muffin tin or ramekins

Preheat the oven to 350 °F (180 °C).
Whisk together the coconut milk, cream cheese, cocoa powder, erythritol and egg until no longer lumpy. Pour the batter into two small baking tins and bake in the oven for 7 minutes. Open the oven door and place a spoonful of cold nut paste in the middle of the muffins. Press the nut paste down until it's just submerged (see tip). Bake for another 10 minutes or until the cakes are cooked through.

Tip: nut paste
There are several different types of nut pastes available. Some contain more carbs than others. I use almond nut paste: it contains about 6 grams carbs per 100 grams.

Tip: adding cold nut paste after 7 minutes
The only reason why we put the nut paste in later is to prevent it from sinking to the bottom. It gives a nice effect when the nut paste ends up in the middle once the cakes are done. Make sure the nut paste is cool from the fridge so it's still firm and you can press a cube of nut paste into the cake. Warm nut paste drips and is harder to work with.

Per serving: 7.2g P (18.6%) / 1.8g NetC (4.5%) / 13.3g F (76.9%)

Chocolate cookies

Preparation time: 15 minutes – Cooking time: 15 minutes

Makes about 8 cookies

3 ½ oz (100 g) ground almonds
1 ½ oz (40 g) coconut oil
1 egg white from a large egg
¼ teaspoon baking soda (see tip)
1 ½ oz dark chocolate, 100% cocoa (see tip)
1 oz (30 g) erythritol

Extra: baking parchment

Deliciously chewy cookies to go with your coffee or tea.

Preheat the oven to 350 °F (180 °C).
Coarsely chop the chocolate. Melt the coconut oil.
Combine the ground almonds with the egg white, erythritol and baking soda. Add the melted coconut oil followed by the coarsely chopped chocolate.

Line a baking sheet with baking parchment and heap spoonfuls of the mixture onto the parchment. Flatten them slightly with the back of a spoon.
Bake in the oven for 15 to 20 minutes or until the cookies turn golden brown.

Tip: chocolate

Choose unsweetened chocolate made from 100% cocoa or at least 95% cocoa.
Check the ingredients on the package: chocolate made from 90% cocoa has a 10% sugar content, 85% cocoa has 15% sugar and so on ... Too much sugar for a ketogenic diet.

Tip: baking soda

I prefer to use baking soda, which is an ingredient in baking powder. It's a pure product that only requires an acid such as cider vinegar, yogurt, buttermilk (which contains lactic acid), lemon or lime juice, cocoa, egg whites ... to achieve the same results as baking powder. One spoonful of baking soda corresponds to about three spoonfuls of baking powder.

Per cookie: 4.1g P (10.5%) / 1.3g NetC (3.3%) / 14.5g F (86.2%)

Coffee-flavored chocolate mousse

Preparation time: 20 minutes – Cooking time: none

2 tablespoons (½ oz/15 g) cocoa powder
1 ¾ oz (50 g) coconut milk
1 oz + ⅓ oz (30 g + 10 g) dark chocolate, 100% cocoa (or >90% unsweetened chocolate)
1 level teaspoonful instant coffee
3 ½ oz (100 g) cream
1 to 2 teaspoons erythritol to taste

Melt 1 oz (30 g) of chocolate in the oven at 175 °F (50 °C). First, combine the cocoa powder with the coconut milk, erythritol and instant coffee and stir everything together well until you have a smooth paste. Beat the cream until peaks form. Stir the cocoa mixture into the cream. Using a mixer, beat the cream again until stiff peaks form. Stir in the melted chocolate. Divide the mousse into glasses. Coarsely chop the leftover chocolate and sprinkle over the mousse to garnish. Keep the mousse in the fridge until it's ready to be served.

Per serving: 4.6g P (4.8%) / 6g NetC (6.4%) / 37g F (88.8%)

*A frothy chocolate mousse
for coffee lovers,
for a touch of variety.*

Luscious baked cream

Preparation time: 25 minutes (without base: 10 minutes) – Cooking time: 30 minutes

A delightful dessert.

For the cream
2 egg yolks (see tip)
9 oz (250 g) Philadelphia cream cheese
1 ¼ oz (40 g) erythritol
a few drops of vanilla extract
lemon zest

For the base
2 oz (60 g) ground almonds
½ oz (15 g) butter
1 teaspoon ground ginger
1 egg white (see tip)
1 teaspoon erythritol

Extra: baking dish or cake tin (about 6 inches/16 cm across) and baking parchment

Preheat the oven to 350 °F (180 °C).

First, make the base:
Melt the butter and stir all the ingredients into the butter.
We only use one egg white for the base; we will add the egg yolks to the cream later.
Line the cake tin with baking parchment and fill the tin with the mixture. Flatten with the back of a spoon. Bake in the oven for 15 to 20 minutes or until the base browns nicely.

For the cream:
Whisk the cream cheese together with 2 egg yolks (this includes the egg yolk that you have left over from the base). Add the erythritol, vanilla essence and lemon zest.
Combine well. Pour the cream over the base and return to the oven for another 20 minutes.

Tip: baking dish or cake tin?
I lined a baking dish 6 inches in diameter and 1 ½ inches deep with parchment paper. You can also use a small springform cake tin.

Tip: eggs
You'll need two eggs for this recipe. Use 2 egg yolks for the cream and one egg white for the base. You can throw away the second egg white or use it for something else.

Tip: in a hurry?
When I don't have much time, I don't make the base and put the cream into small ramekins without the baking parchment. And then I bake them in the oven for about 20 minutes. I serve the cream in the ramekins with a spoon ... A wonderful treat, and so easy to make!

Per serving: 19.3g P (12.8%) / 6.8g NetC (4.5%) / 55.2g F (82.7%)

AVOCADOS ON THE COVER

Have a look at the basket with the avocados on the cover. You have to admit, the avocado is a beautiful and very photogenic fruit. But that's not the only reason they grace the cover of this book. The avocado is also a quintessential keto fruit, rich in fats and fiber —a unique combination for a plant-based product. And it's rich in vitamins B, C, K, and potassium. In short, an exceptionally healthy fruit and an ideal ingredient for a keto cure.

It's actually a large berry; a fruit, in other words, but we often treat avocado as a vegetable. The avocado is one of nature's most versatile gifts, but also a delicate one. It's an exotic fruit, an import from the South. And, as with all exotic agricultural produce, avocados are a double-edged sword. Avocados require plenty of water to grow and their extensive cultivation often leads to rampant deforestation. Thankfully, that's not always the case. I was recently in Peru, where I met a small-scale avocado farmer. There was enough water in the region, and he grew avocados in an ecologically sustainable way. But sadly, he couldn't export his fruits because he couldn't compete with the large international producers. He sold his avocados for market prices at the local market. I also saw many Peruvians selling their own avocados by the roadside.

Most large supermarket chains are also looking for avocados that are grown in an ecologically sustainable way in areas where water shortage is not an issue. I would say, if you are environmentally conscious about these things, find products that come from regions where resources, such as water, are abundant. If you don't want to eat avocados at all or are allergic to them, replace them with a mixture of cooked broccoli and mascarpone, a delicious alternative.

The key message is that we need to take care with this divine fruit and use it sparingly. For example, I only eat avocado when it is ripe. That means I don't have to throw a single avocado away. And above all, I don't have to eat avocados all the time, but when I do eat them, I value them for the divine fruit they are.

EXTRA

INDEX

www.purepascale.com
www.pascalenaessens.com
www.lannoo.com

Have you had good experiences with this way of eating? We'd love to hear about it. Visit the website mentioned above and send us a message via the "contact" page. You can read more stories under the header "testimonials". United we stand!

RECIPES, STYLING AND CONCEPT
Pascale Naessens

TEXTS
Pascale Naessens, Hanno Pijl, William Cortvriendt

ENGLISH TRANSLATION
Textcase, Deventer

RECIPE MACRONUTRIENT CALCULATIONS
Dietician Sabrina Mattens

PHOTOGRAPHY
Roos Mestdagh, Diego Fransens, Ramon De LLano

DESIGN
Leen Depooter – quod. voor de vorm.

If you have any comments or questions, please do not hesitate to contact the publisher:
redactielifestyle@lannoo.be

D/2022/45/119 – NUR 440-441
ISBN: 978 94 014 8223 3

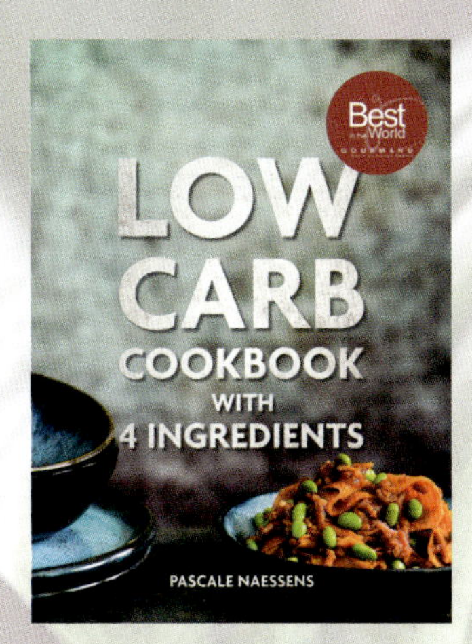

Low carb Cookbook 1

ISBN 978 9 4014 6148 1

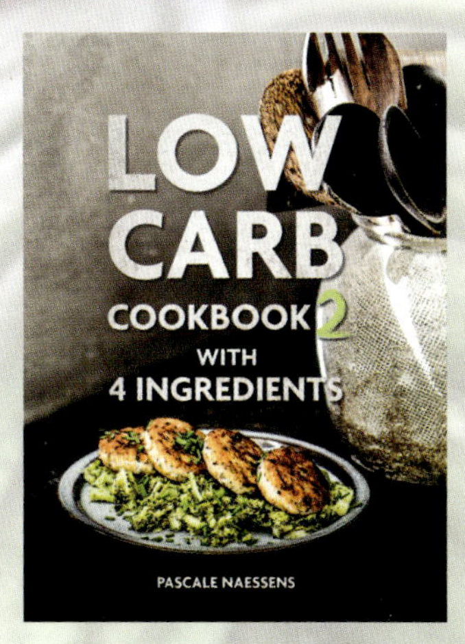

Low carb Cookbook 2

ISBN 978 94 014 6841 1

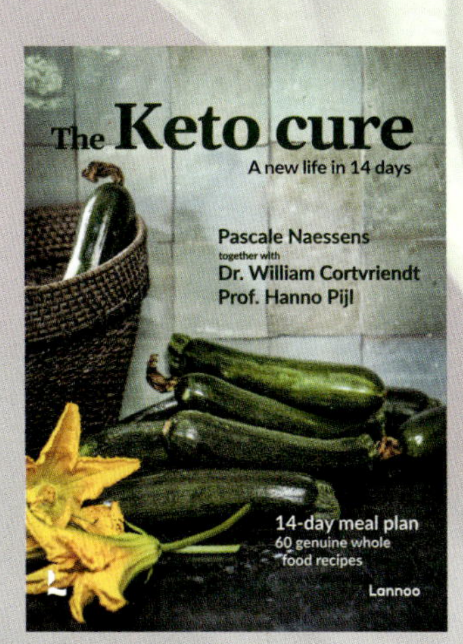

The Keto cure 1

ISBN 978 94 014 7419 1

Natural food

ISBN 978 94 014 1983 3